About Island Press

Since 1984, the nonprofit organization Island Press has been stimulating, shaping, and communicating ideas that are essential for solving environmental problems worldwide. With more than 1,000 titles in print and some 30 new releases each year, we are the nation's leading publisher on environmental issues. We identify innovative thinkers and emerging trends in the environmental field. We work with world-renowned experts and authors to develop cross-disciplinary solutions to environmental challenges.

Island Press designs and executes educational campaigns, in conjunction with our authors, to communicate their critical messages in print, in person, and online using the latest technologies, innovative programs, and the media. Our goal is to reach targeted audiences—scientists, policy makers, environmental advocates, urban planners, the media, and concerned citizens—with information that can be used to create the framework for long-term ecological health and human well-being.

Island Press gratefully acknowledges major support from The Bobolink Foundation, Caldera Foundation, The Curtis and Edith Munson Foundation, The Forrest C. and Frances H. Lattner Foundation, The JPB Foundation, The Kresge Foundation, The Summit Charitable Foundation, Inc., and many other generous organizations and individuals.

The opinions expressed in this book are those of the author(s) and do not necessarily reflect the views of our supporters.

The Food Sharing Revolution

The Food Sharing Revolution

HOW START-UPS, POP-UPS, AND CO-OPS
ARE CHANGING THE WAY WE EAT

Michael S. Carolan

ISLANDPRESS

Washington | Covelo | London

ISLAND PRESS is a trademark of the Center for Resource Economics.

Library of Congress Control Number: 2018941933

All Island Press books are printed on environmentally responsible materials.

Manufactured in the United States of America
10 9 8 7 6 5 4 3 2 1

Keywords: collaborative consumption, platform cooperativism, food sovereignty, food justice, co-op, community supported agriculture (CSA), agribusiness, sustainable agriculture, Uber, Airbnb.

Contents

Acknowledgments

Airports are curious places. People coming and going, nameless faces attached to rushing bodies—rushing, often, so they can be among the first to wait. I was having one of these waits recently at Denver International Airport when I heard my name and felt a hand placed on my arm. I turned, saw a thin arm, and followed it down to a bony wrist, out of which sprang bluish veins beneath papery skin. I looked up and recognized the face that peered back at me. It belonged to someone whom I had interviewed for this book. The manuscript had been written, at least a first draft, so I was able to outline its contents while we waited together, making sure to repeatedly thank her for her earlier willingness to be interviewed.

Most of what I know, I know because people have been incredibly generous with their time. As I like to tell people, I earned my *real* degree interviewing people, after getting my PhD.

I wish I could express personally my gratitude, punctuated with a handshake or hug, to everyone who gave to this project. Thanks to everyone who donated their time to be interviewed for *The Food Sharing Revolution*. Time is precious; I realize that. I hope I have respected that gift by accurately recounting your stories.

I owe no less gratitude to Emily Turner. I continue to learn by the grace of your experience and writing wisdom.

Who I am, and why I'm interested in food, can be traced directly to my parents and to my very small town (350 people strong!) upbringing. Food and agriculture are issues that have been deeply personal for me for as long as I can remember. Mom and Dad: thanks for that.

Nora, Elena, and Joey. For you, this project meant numerous nights away from Dad and days of Mom having to do the parenting of two. This is really one of those situations where words of thanks just don't do justice. So: thanks. And also: *sorry*, as I realize I can't give you those lost hours back. I might have been away, but you were always with me.

I also want to thank the following institutions and professional networks that supported this project in their own unique ways: Colorado State University (United States); Korea University (Korea); the Australasian Agri-Food Research Network; Otago University (New Zealand); the University of Auckland (New Zealand), the University of Toronto (Canada), and the Toronto Food Policy Council (Canada).

Parts of this project were supported by the National Institute of Food and Agriculture (grant number COL00725) and by the National Research Foundation of Korea (NRF-2016S1A3A2924243).

Ownership through Sharing

You know it's hot when you can see it. Standing alongside a field just off Route 2 in Massachusetts, I was mesmerized by the heat rising off the road, blurring the horizon far in the distance. The bright midday sun beat down on the top of my head. The thermometer in my rental, a mid-size whose air-conditioning made more noise than cold air, read 103.

I was driving to meet Josh, a first-generation dairy farmer on his thousand-plus acres of land. We almost had to cancel because of the heat. Not because Josh was cowed by the triple-digit weather but because one of his giant barn fans—a lifesaver on hot days—needed immediate attention. He managed to get the fan fixed in short order, telling me something about how it needed a new belt. Fortunately, he had plenty in reserve.

I wanted to connect with Josh because his enterprise is an anomaly compared with others in the state. He's in his early forties—a young pup in a profession with an average age approaching sixty. And when we talked, he had roughly five years of experience under his belt. The percentage of farms in the United States operated by individuals who have been in the profession less than a decade has been in decline for decades. The figure is now around 20 percent, down from close to 40 percent in 1982.

Josh remarked at one point during our interview, with a tone that sounded both incredulous and profoundly sad, "Within another ten years the average farmer is going to be eligible for Medicare—*Medicare*." Josh mentioned land prices repeatedly as he tried to explain why he's the exception and not the rule. In Massachusetts, farmland sells for an average of $10,400 per acre. In its push to support new farmers, the U.S. Department of Agriculture lends them up to $300,000 to get started, sufficient for a couple dozen acres of land or a new tractor. "It's not nearly enough," Josh flatly told me.

Josh was lucky, by his own admission, and grateful. While he was telling me how he "made it," his face lit up with an ear-to-ear grin, bright even in the blazing sun. Josh doesn't own his land, his seeds, or even all of his equipment. And the cows: not his, either. His business model rests on a mix of sharing and cooperative arrangements. "Property's a burden," he explained, adding, "Through sharing, I have more control over my life and business." This remarkable statement, which stands opposed to principles that lie at the core of American democracy, got me thinking.

Thomas Jefferson must be turning in his grave. Perhaps he is making room for his vision of agrarian democracy. This ideal, which takes as sacrosanct the role of individual landownership in ensuring a republic of free and prosperous citizens, has since expanded, romanticizing sole ownership throughout foodscapes. Business ownership comes with privileges, to quote the title of a recent *Forbes* article.[1] Except when it doesn't, especially for those entrepreneurs without an angel investor looking over their shoulder.

As food becomes a corporate enterprise, two things are happening to the Jeffersonian ideal. First, individual ownership is becoming further out of reach for many. Gone are the days of the government giving away land to settlers—160 acres, thanks to the Homestead Act of 1862—in exchange for five years of continuous residence. Today, land is expensive, just like everything about farming—equipment, refrigeration trucks, semitrucks and trailers, inputs, even seed. Farmland inflation rates have increased by roughly 150 percent in the past fifteen years, propelling the price of ground in some states north of $13,000 per acre.[2] In the meantime, U.S. farmers saw a 45 percent drop in net farm income between 2013 and 2016, with the USDA expecting incomes to drop by another 8.7 percent in 2017.[3] If you do an Internet search for "U.S. farm incomes," you might read that farm household incomes rose between 2015 and 2016—cue in on "household," as those figures include off-farm income. I expect farm household incomes to rise as family members are forced to find jobs elsewhere, though I'm not sure that is something we ought to be celebrating.

Small businesses are not finding things any easier, as most struggle even to get off the ground. Roughly 60 percent of all restaurants fail within the first year, with nearly 80 percent shuttering before celebrating their five-year anniversary.[4] Restaurants with twenty or fewer employees fare even worse.[5]

Food safety laws assume restaurants either are chains or are bankrolled like them. Want to start a business and cook out of your home? If that is even legal—it isn't in many instances—you are looking at a major kitchen upgrade: stainless steel countertops, triple-compartment sinks, adequate mechanical ventilation to the outside (in your bathroom too, in many states), proper signage (e.g., No Smoking), and on and on. Good luck financing those upgrades with interest rates in the double, in some cases *triple*, digits. You know things are bad when credit cards become *the* source of capital for many aspiring food entrepreneurs.

The second change concerns those who have done it, who can declare, "It's mine." For them, the ideal can feel more like a nightmare. Buying seed no longer guarantees ownership. Patents and contracts with seed companies prevent farmers from reselling seed or even saving some for a future season. Farmers can't even fix their own tractors—*their own tractors*. They are still allowed to change tires and fix belts; no problem. Yet the moment this tinkering involves the tractor's computer "brain," which, let's face it, is a bridge too far for most anyway, owners enter murky legal waters.

Why are farmers getting the short end of the stick? For the same reason most food entrepreneurs are, and eaters too. We lack a meaningful say in how the entire system is organized. The Jeffersonian ideal: an ideological weapon of mass distraction. It operates by focusing our attention on the individual ownership of *stuff*—tractors, seed, land, health inspector approved kitchen space, and so on—while ownership of the *foodscape* is systematically being taken from us, becoming concentrated in the hands of a few. Even when farmers own their land and buildings, they have lost control of most everything else. For that, we can thank such things as contract farming and market concentration in those sectors farmers buy from (e.g., seed companies) and sell to (e.g., meat processors).

These barriers and pitfalls to ownership mean that large corporations thoroughly dominate the foodscape. And though family farms continue to exist, the demographics of the sector look nothing like the general population, even though there are countless want-to-be farmers—of practically every race, creed, and color—waiting on the sidelines. Our having been seduced by the idea of individual ownership means we need to accept our own culpability for what comes next: low wages, obesity, antibiotic resistance, food waste, hunger, and other delights of an industrialized system. Is it time to consider a different model?

The sharing economy, which also goes by such names as collaborative consumption and platform cooperativism, offers a real alternative. You have probably heard of Uber and Airbnb—the former term is now used as a verb. Such platforms have captured our attention and imagination because they facilitate sharing among networks broader than our grandparents could ever have imagined. While previous generations of farmers shared seed, they did so largely with neighbors or acquaintances. Smartphones, algorithms, GPS data, and cloud computing—in a word, *technology*—have changed things considerably. To quote liberally from the *Economist*:

> Technology has reduced transaction costs, making sharing assets cheaper and easier than ever—and therefore possible on a much larger scale. The big change is the availability of more data about people and things, which allows physical assets to be disaggregated and consumed as services. Before the internet, renting a surfboard, a power tool or a parking space from someone else was feasible, but was usually more trouble than it was worth. Now websites such as Airbnb, RelayRides and SnapGoods match up owners and renters; smartphones with GPS let people see where the nearest rentable car is parked; social networks provide a way to check up on people and build trust; and online payment systems handle the billing.[6]

In short, technology has made sharing easier, allowing collaborative arrangements to challenge the dominant industrial system. Which is not to say that technology holds all the answers—there's a value to face-to-face encounters that gets lost in the sea of digital communication. In this book, I'll explore both old-fashioned and high-tech models of sharing, looking at the costs and benefits. My primary interest in sharing technologies is that they have prompted a conversation about the way our food economy functions, opening up space for more equitable and humane relationships.

By the halfway mark through our interview, Josh had shown me the dairy parlor and machine shed. We had just taken refuge under a grand red maple, resting our hind ends on upturned paint pails that had been repurposed to haul feed. The teenage son of a co-owner was mowing lawn in the distance on a John Deere riding tractor. Barn swallows feasted on insects that had taken flight, their cool bunker disturbed by a forty-eight-inch blade traveling at some three thousand rotations per minute. For a good minute, our attention was captivated by countless swallows diving, climbing, and crossing between the wires of a nearby clothesline—nature's Blue Angels minus the noise and contrails.

Josh's farm is cooperatively owned. "Cooperatively owned, cooperatively managed, cooperatively profited from," was how Josh put it, which nicely summed up its legal status. This was not an enterprise consisting of multiple independent farm businesses working on shared land.

"We're better farmers because we farm together. This is a model that can feed the world." During our brief time together, I had come to know Josh as a modest person. He was quick to deflect praise, for instance, to his partners and wife. So the statement caught me off guard. There was an intensity in his eyes, burning like brown topaz, that I had not seen before. *He is serious,* I remember thinking.

After turning slightly on his pail to face me, and wiping his forehead with a handkerchief, he explained himself. I had heard many of the story's elements before. There was the bit about how "the world needs more food," followed by a shout-out to "economies of scale."

Was I being fed the standard line about the necessity of industrial farming?

Not quite.

Josh and his collaborators own collectively more than one thousand acres, about half in pasture. It would be a difficult farm to manage by yourself, in light of the sustainable techniques used: rotational grazing (i.e., systematically moving cows from one fenced pen, called a paddock, to another based on "the look of the grass"); integrated pest management techniques (i.e., using good insects to eat the bad ones); and USDA certified organic methods. Each requires a deep knowledge of agroecology. To make his point, Josh began ticking off names of native plants that his cows especially like; each paddock, roughly fifty acres, has a unique mix. "It's a lot of ground to keep track of," he told me, just before explaining how he literally gets down on his hands and knees to measure grass length and soil compaction levels.

While Josh talked about economies of scale, he was also quick to mention diseconomies of scale—the idea that you really can have too much of a good thing. He explained repeatedly that farms have gotten "too big," pointing out that "when you're farming in excess of a thousand acres, by yourself, you can't possibly implement the management practices that we do here."

With the mower approaching, we shared a look, stood, and walked toward the house. When we'd moved an additional twenty feet away from the John Deere, Josh stopped and faced me. "Imagine a scenario where we didn't share. We each would need to have our own equipment, our own buildings, our own grain bins, trucks, four-wheelers, milking parlors. It wouldn't be economically feasible. We'd have to get bigger to afford it all, which means we'd have to be at each other's throats trying to buy each other out."

It wasn't just about the economic benefits that came with sharing stuff. Josh talked about how he and his collaborators had gained leverage as sellers. While most farmers have to take the price they are offered because of market concentration in the processing and retail sectors, Josh can actually negotiate the price of his milk and meat.

As for that comment about how sharing animals, land, and equipment can feed the world: it was aspirational, but the reality is not beyond our grasp.

"Think of it. If our neighbors did this, and their neighbors, and their neighbors' neighbors, this model would be scalable." There were those dancing brown topaz eyes again. "This is about scaling *out*, not up." "Scaling up" has come to mean independent farm businesses getting bigger while pushing out competitors. "Scaling out" can mean something profoundly different—farmers actually collaborating. If by scaling out farmers can also reclaim their lost negotiating power in a marketplace that has become thoroughly dominated by corporate agriculture, then sign me up for this vision.

Cooperatives such as Josh's are just one example of the food sharing economy in action. Sharing can occur at any point in the process of growing, processing, cooking, selling, and eating food, and it may or may not involve new technology. This book describes a number of web based sharing platforms designed to facilitate exchanges. Some allow chefs to cook in their homes by coordinating orders and deliveries; one allows farmers to share—though, if you ask me, "rent" is a more apt descriptor—their tractors; another connects aspiring food entrepreneurs with idle kitchen space; a few even facilitate peer-to-peer loans.

Then there's the case of FoodCloud, a platform designed to recover food that would otherwise go to waste. The nonprofit company, which goes by the same name as its platform, is based in Ireland. With its software, retailers upload details about food that is nearing its sell-by date or is deemed too ugly to spend good money on. (The Food and Agriculture Organization of the United Nations calculates that cosmetic standards in the retail industry exclude up to 40 percent of fresh produce from the market—that's 800–900 million tons of food annually, or the equivalent of 9,000 Nimitz-class aircraft carriers.)[7] At the other end, local charities receive automatic alerts asking if they wish to collect the food and distribute it to those in need. Tesco Ireland uses the platform in all of its 140 stores. In May 2016, Aldi announced its national partnership with FoodCloud. By November of that year, the retailer's 79 participating stores reported donating over 500,000 meals (234 metric tons of food) thanks to this relationship.[8]

In this book, you will also learn about seed libraries, which are reminiscent of the wildly successful free seed program implemented by the U.S. federal government from 1819 to 1924. By 1900, 1 billion free packages of seed were being mailed to farmers annually. Today, seed libraries are illegal in some states. In one egregious case, a Pennsylvania county commissioner managed to drop the t-bomb—agro-*terrorism*—when describing why she was against them. Fortunately, a seed library movement is under way. I tell about some of its successes and why more of these libraries are needed so future generations can reclaim ownership of their foodscapes through seeds and the communities that sustain them.

Approximately 45 percent of all U.S. farmland (that's close to 400 million acres) is rented. Nearly all goes to supporting the status quo: large-scale, which typically means conventional, agriculture. One landlord explained it to me this way: "If I'm going to make the same whether I lease my land"—he rents out more than a thousand acres of prime Iowa farmland—"to a dozen small-scale beginning farmers or to one established large grower, I'm going to take that one lease. It's just easier for me." Fair enough. But if growers interested in supporting alternative foodscapes do not have access to land, we have a real problem. Collaborative based alternatives to renting are beginning to flourish, giving individuals from diverse socioeconomic backgrounds an opportunity to acquire ownership of their farms without individually owning (or renting) them. The stories told here involve land cooperatives, crowdfunding platforms that give eaters and farmers a shared stake in their foodscape, and inventive community based trusts.

Speaking of crowdfunding: the total volume of loans held by community banks peaked in 2008, only to drop precipitously with the Great Recession, bottoming out in 2011. Enter peer-to-peer lending platforms, especially those focused on connecting peers from within the same community. More than just providing access to low interest financing for aspiring entrepreneurs, community based lending encourages a moral economy. Such platforms represent a departure from the dog-eat-dog—or, in the case of food companies, eaters-get-diabetes-shareholders-get-rich—business model common throughout conventional foodscapes. Here, you will read accounts of borrowers and lenders being matched up within the same community; of lenders who frequent the business their loan is supporting and who rally family and friends to do the same; of borrowers who have met, repeatedly, the person or persons at the other end of the loan; and of onetime borrowers who later choose to become lenders themselves. In other words, you will encounter stories in which peer-to-peer lending has made communities and foodscapes stronger by *bringing people together.*

That's just a taste of what lies ahead.

While the sharing economy holds real promise for making our foodscape more sustainable and just, slapping the label "sharing" on an enterprise does not necessarily mean that it is equitable. While many sharing platforms claim to be fighting for the little guy, at every turn projecting an image of David taking on the Goliath monopolists, the reality can be far different. Take what many consider to be the archetypal sharing model: Uber.

Chances are good that you are familiar with Uber, even if you haven't used it to get to the airport or home from a bar. For those living under a rock: Uber facilitates peer-to-peer ride sharing for a fee—the company keeps 20–30 percent of each fare. Launched in 2010, Uber reached its first billion rides in 2015, a total it saw doubled just six months later. In the summer of 2017, another milestone was announced: 5 billion trips worldwide.

One study found that the average Uber driver makes $364 per month, among the highest incomes among the sharing platforms surveyed.[9] Another study tried to calculate the average hourly wage for Uber drivers. Researchers arrived at $15.68 per hour before factoring in expenses such as gas, maintenance, and depreciation.[10] Other analyses, meanwhile, paint a far less optimistic financial picture after calculating for taxes that an employer would otherwise pay, namely Social Security and Medicare, which drivers owe under the Self-Employment Contributions Act of 1954.[11]

While some of these findings may appear heartening, others should dampen our enthusiasm. The people who provide services through many of these sharing platforms tend to be highly educated, and many even report having well paying full-time jobs.[12] For them, driving for Uber is supplemental income. There's nothing wrong with that per se, except that they are crowding out workers who depend on the income of service jobs. These are tasks traditionally performed by people who have not gone to college and who come from lower socioeconomic households. Generally, people with PhDs who make more than $100,000 per year do not drive taxis on the side. But some of them may drive for Uber.

In some cases, sharing platforms might be pushing out those whom the sole ownership economy has already placed in a precarious position, perhaps even making them more vulnerable.

Then there is the corporation itself. Uber's business tactics are legend. In many ways, the business is the closest embodiment of Nietzschean will to power since the days of the robber barons, when Andrew Carnegie and John D. Rockefeller's style of unrestrained capitalism crushed anything daring to stand in its way. It has been reported, for example, that Uber has assigned its internet protocol to the tax haven of Bermuda, leaving less than 2 percent of its net revenue taxable by the U.S. government.[13] So with one hand it takes jobs away from the already vulnerable while with the other it hides its money overseas, robbing government programs of their tax base.

A few years back, Casey Newton reported on Uber's questionable business practices in the *Verge*, uncovering a special project with the code name Operation SLOG—Supplying Long-term Operations Growth.[14] Employees, or "sloggers," equipped with burner phones, credit cards, and recruitment kits, were instructed to take rides with Lyft drivers and try to convince them to switch to Uber. If sloggers learned that they had already tried to recruit the driver, they immediately canceled the ride. There were more than five thousand cancellations during the initial months of this poaching campaign. Couple this street-thug capitalist mentality with a bankroll north of a *billion* dollars and you should begin to understand why I am reluctant to hand my and my children's future over to Uber.

What happens when this brand of creative annihilation crushes its competition, local taxi companies, Lyft, Grab (in Southeast Asia), Ola (in India), all of them, the world over? Über Uber. A company with that cultural DNA is not going to let its workers unionize. With its drivers having nowhere else to go, Uber would be well positioned to start taking an even bigger commission. (In the past few years, its original 20 percent commission rate has crept up to, in some markets, 30 percent.)[15] Just wait until there are self-driving cars, when today's well paid drivers become tomorrow's latest Uber roadkill—industry insiders are expecting this fatality to take place around 2030.[16] At the other end of the transaction, there will be little to stop the company from charging surge rates at every opportunity: "Oh, it's sprinkling; factor in a surge at 2.5x!"

Squeeze workers. Squeeze consumers. It is what monopolists have always done. *Every one of them.*

The media, talking heads, and our youth are continually touting the "sharing economy" as the next big thing.[17] (Those aged eighteen to twenty-four are nearly twice as likely as those twenty-five and older to say that access is the new ownership.) So how do we ensure it is a gentle giant, not the 800-pound gorilla of capitalism, that empowers successful farmers like Josh rather than putting taxi drivers out of work? How can we use it to retool and reboot the Jeffersonian ideal, creating a more equitable and sustainable foodscape?

We need to differentiate between types of sharing. Uber and the cooperative partnership that Josh is part of are different. That much is obvious. But how do we talk about those distinctions?

My goal has been to learn from those actively engaged in the food sharing economy. I conducted more than two hundred face-to-face interviews with people doing precisely that, plus a few dozen more interviews with people getting the short end of the individual ownership stick.[18] By around interview one hundred, it had become clear that all these various practices could be placed into one of three buckets. Some practices involved creating *access* to material things. Others focused on creating and exchanging *knowledge*. Still others were centered on building *community*. And some did all these things to various degrees.

The remaining chapters are organized around these three themes. After the next two chapters, which discuss why the Jeffersonian dream has turned out to be a nightmare, chapters are organized by what the platforms explicitly purport to share: chapters 3 and 4 discuss those promising to facilitate access to stuff; chapters 5 and 6 are about those exchanging knowledge; and chapters 7 and 8 illustrate examples of building community.

As you will also quickly learn, these buckets are porous. Luckily for us, most of the platforms examined shared in more ways than one, though some did prove to be little more than one-shot wonders, delivering exactly what they advertised. This book is not about Uber. But for illustration purposes, I would place the platform in the one-shot wonder category. You get what you pay for—a ride—and not much else.

Collaborative exchanges that incorporate all three elements have the most potential to afford food sovereignty. The term, popularized in 1996 at the World Food Summit in Rome by the international peasants' movement La Vía Campesina, a movement some two hundred million strong, emphasizes the importance of personal agency, social justice, and cooperation.[19] La Vía Campesina's full definition of "food sovereignty" is "the right of peoples to healthy and culturally appropriate food produced through ecologically sound and sustainable methods, and their right to define their own food and agriculture systems. It puts those who produce, distribute and consume food at the heart of food systems and policies rather than the demands of markets and corporations."[20] At heart, this is a deeply democratic vision of how to feed the world. This vision stands opposed to the status quo, in which the monopolists work to hold, well, a monopoly on what, how, and with whom we eat.[21]

The final chapter discusses in detail what it means to practice sharing that affords individuals and communities food sovereignty. Examples, however, are scattered throughout the book. That's good news—food sovereignty can take many forms. Sovereignty can bloom a thousand times, in different forms, fields, and environments.

To highlight one example that fits into each of the three buckets, take the Food Corridor. Discussed further in chapter 3, the Food Corridor is a business headquartered in Fort Collins, Colorado. (It sounds weird saying "headquartered" when you're talking about a company with three employees, one communications person, and three cofounders.) The company matches idle commercial kitchens with aspiring entrepreneurs through software, charging users a monthly membership fee. As of September 2017, the Food Corridor had customers in twenty-six states.

The cost of a commercial kitchen, as you might guess, is prohibitive. Colorado has the Cottage Foods Act, a law that first came into effect in 2012. Similar to laws found in other states, the act allows very small scale operations to test the commercial waters by producing things like apple sauce or cookies in their homes for direct-to-consumer sales within the state without licensing or inspection. But because the act applies only to "non–potentially hazardous" foods—basically those that do not require refrigeration—and has a cap of $5,000 in net sales per product, most start-ups have to play by the same rules and face the same hurdles as chains do. And above all, they need M-O-N-E-Y—a lot of it. Being able to rent otherwise idle commercial kitchen space is thus a potential game changer.

To say the Food Corridor offers access only to stuff misses a great deal. According to CEO Ashley Colpaart, "the long-term goal is to be a [decentralized] incubator, for start-ups, for communities, even. More than providing access to space, we want to create resilient food systems."[22] The goal is more vision than reality at the moment. But it isn't all talk. The Food Corridor launched the Network for Incubator and Commissary Kitchens in March 2016 as a Facebook group, which currently hosts approximately nine hundred members. This network of food activists, entrepreneurs, and practitioners shares data, best practices, and technical assistance to build vibrant communities through successful shared-use kitchen businesses. These exchanges include support for what is called in the biz "ecosystem services," such as food liability insurance, label printing, and food safety tools. Which is exactly what has to take place if we want to dislodge old ways of thinking and habits rooted in an individual ownership ethos. If you have questions about, say, shared-use kitchen businesses, but the people with "answers" know only the status quo, why would we expect anything to change?

As a company, the Food Corridor accomplished much in identifying and legitimizing the shared-use kitchen sector in its first two years of existence. But "success" has multiple meanings among those looking to shake things up. I would expect those involved to continue to innovate, in ways that create cost efficiencies for users and social synergies among those inhabiting this shared ecosystem. Food sovereignty is not about one-size-fits-all solutions. That thinking is what got us into this mess: the belief that there is one pathway to prosperity. The Green Revolution. Tax cuts. "Get big or get out!" Here is a piece of advice: a solution that can fit on a bumper sticker probably isn't much of one. Sovereignty *is* about supporting diverse individuals and enterprises; it's about building networks based on the idea that we are stronger together—where independence is born of interdependence.

As opposed to the Uber monoculture, those behind the Food Corridor let discrepancies across foodscapes bloom. Ashley reaffirmed repeatedly the company's commitment to social enterprises and nonprofits, though Food Corridor customers include for-profit entities as well. That commitment is evidenced in how the company works closely with individual users to learn about their "pain points"—those costs that the software platform might ease. This conversation has on a number of occasions resulted in the Food Corridor customizing its software. A one-size-fits-all platform might work for the Olive Gardens of the world, and it has certainly worked wonders for Uber. Small-scale food entrepreneurs, meanwhile, especially those working within underserved communities or with underserved populations, have unique needs and challenges. Exchanges supported by Food Corridor–enabled ecosystems allow these entrepreneurial polycultures to survive and in some cases thrive. This is significant for businesses trying to make their way in a world that privileges individual ownership and rewards cutthroat—or, as Josh put it, "at each other's throats"—behavior.

When a flower doesn't bloom, you fix the environment in which it grows, not the flower.[23] But also, by changing that environment you will discover mutations and varieties that wouldn't have sprouted under the prior conditions. The Food Corridor is helping to change the environment, and in the process, it is redefining "business as usual."

By highlighting efforts such as the Food Corridor and Josh's cooperative, I set out to examine what constitutes *true* ownership. In these pages, we will explore what it will take to have real choice about the products we make and eat, the kinds of lives we lead, and the direction of our communities. Can we work collaboratively to create healthy and prosperous foodscapes? Is there a new path to the American dream?

Yes, and yes.

CHAPTER 1

A Nightmare Realized

Born and raised in Iowa, I spent many summers working for my dad. He was a high school science teacher and a house and barn painter over the summer. He painted, he would jokingly tell people, so he could afford to teach. He still paints, even after retiring from teaching. (He would probably tell you he now paints to afford retirement.) There was one guy—Marvin—who had us paint his farm buildings every six or seven years. He was one of *those* farmers: kept his field rows neat and tidy, mowed ditches between the road and his crops, string trimmed fence lines, and took pride in having well maintained buildings.

I had the opportunity to visit Marvin during a recent trip back to the Hawkeye State. From the road, everything on his farm looked as I remembered. The buildings were still immaculate. "That's one thing I can still control, when and what color they get painted," he told me. Judging by that quote, you might be able to guess that something was amiss with Marvin's operation.

"I didn't sign up for this," were the first words out of his mouth when I asked him how things were going. My earliest memories of Marvin date back to the early 1980s, when the farmhouse was new, furnished with the first VHS machine that I had ever seen. My sense at the time was that Marvin was rich. He wasn't, though he admitted during our recent visit that "times then were a lot better, *a lot* better."

Like many farmers, Marvin has seen his income steadily drop over the past decades. While average U.S. farm incomes have been eroding for generations, the rate of decline has picked up in recent years, falling 36 percent in 2015 and another 14.6 percent in 2016.[1] *Why* Marvin has seen revenues drop is a complicated story.

When describing what he "didn't sign up for," Marvin talked about what it felt like to be on the losing side of both selling and buying power. His takeaway point: there is nothing free, or fair, about the markets that shuttle commodities through conventional foodscapes. Here's a guy who has realized the Jeffersonian dream. He owns most of the land that he cultivates; let's also not forget about those good looking farm buildings. And yet—well, let's just say be careful what you wish for.

Marvin is stuck between a rock and a hard place: the rock being the very small number of firms that supply seed, fertilizer, and pesticides to farmers and the hard place being the highly concentrated market of food processors, manufacturers, and retailers to whom farmers sell. (This phenomenon is not unique to America; figure 1.1 superimposes the conventional foodscapes of the United States and New Zealand.)[2]

To see just how concentrated agricultural markets have become, take a look at a common measure: the four firm concentration ratio—or simply CR4. The CR4 is the sum of market share held by the top four firms in a given sector. A standard rule of thumb is that when the CR4 reaches 20 percent, a market is considered concentrated. Forty percent is highly concentrated. Anything past 60 percent indicates a significantly distorted market. As seen in figure 1.2, there's some serious distortion in the U.S. food market, with rice milling at 85 percent and sugar refining at 95 percent. The level of concentration varies by commodity—the

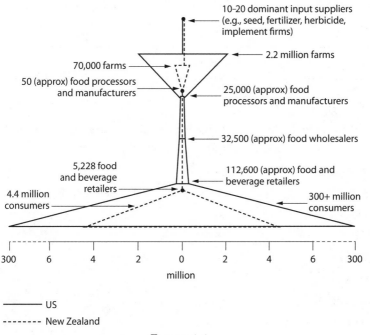

10–20 dominant input suppliers
(e.g., seed, fertilizer, herbicide,
implement firms)

70,000 farms

2.2 million farms

50 (approx) food processors
and manufacturers

25,000 (approx) food
processors and manufacturers

32,500 (approx) food wholesalers

5,228 food
and beverage
retailers

112,600 (approx) food and
beverage retailers

4.4 million
consumers

300+ million
consumers

300   6   4   2   0   2   4   6   300

million

——— US
- - - - - - - New Zealand

FIGURE 1.1

genetically engineered seed market is about as free as markets in North Korea.

Farmers today are dealing with both horizontal and vertical concentration. The CR4 statistic is a measure of *horizontal* concentration, which refers to concentration at one "link" in the food commodity chain. Horizontal integration occurs when firms in the same industry and at the same stage of production merge and dominate a market. *Vertical* concentration, meanwhile, describes the situation in which a single company owns an entire supply chain, as when a meat processor owns the slaughter facilities, hog farms, cornfields, and veterinary services and the transportation to move commodities from one link to the next. This is the situation Marvin finds himself in.

Figure 1.2 Concentration of U.S. agricultural markets (unless otherwise stated)

Sector	CR4*
Beef Slaughter	82%
Beef Production (feedlots)	Top four have one-time feeding capacity of 1.983 million head
Pork Slaughter	63%
Pork Production	Top four have 1.62 million sows in production
Broiler Slaughter	53%
Turkey Slaughter	58%
Animal Feed	44%
Flour Milling	52%
Wet Corn Milling	87%
Soybean Processing	85%
Rice Milling	85%
Cane Sugar Refining	95.0%
GE Corn	CR1 85%
GE Soybean Seed	CR1 92%
GE Cotton Seed	CR1 96%
Farm Equipment	CR3 49% (figure of *global market concentration*)
Big Data Ag. Platforms	*CR6 70%–90% (difficult to calculate)*

* unless otherwise stated

After giving me a tour of his buildings, Marvin plopped down on an old teeter-totter picnic table. (You know the type: one side lifts off the ground unless the weight is evenly distributed across both sides.) We were situated between a new farrowing house and an old but well maintained Quonset hut. With sows squealing in the background, Marvin took a long, deep breath and exhaled. The air rushed between his teeth and made a protracted whistling sound, giving him time to think, either about the actual answer or about the one he wanted to give me. I had inquired about how the business was holding out. Marvin is a proud person. The pause was likely born of reluctance, of his not wanting to risk coming across as complaining about the hand life has dealt him, even to a friend.

It did not come out immediately, but he eventually admitted to feeling "powerless," adding, "The farm is mine, but at the same time it isn't, if that makes sense."

Some of Marvin's angst lay in having made the transition, about ten years back, to contract farming. Before that, he was "a freelance producer of food." Back then, he raised hogs and delivered them to whichever regional market was offering the best spot price on that day—doing what you might think all farmers do in order to sell their wares, if you didn't know better. Things generally don't work like that anymore.

Farming is all about timing, especially in livestock agriculture. Animals need to be sold the moment they reach optimum weight. To wait—to hold out, say, for a better price—is to waste resources (i.e., feed, space) that could be used for fatting up the next herd, litter, flock, brood, or clutch. Dairy producers need to have their bulk tank emptied daily, sometimes every couple of hours. When faced with these realities, farmers cannot hold out for a better price without severely undermining the economics of their operation, to say nothing of their animals' welfare.

Because the market is so concentrated, meat processors have the power to lowball farmers. They know that the Marvins of the world cannot go looking to distant markets for a better price, not when the commodity in question might spoil or even die in the process. Shipping live animals over long distances increases rates of animal mortality. Even if the trip does not kill them, they will almost certainly suffer from what's rather coolly known, given that we're talking about live animals, as "carcass shrinkage."

It was not long before Marvin told me about the terms of his contract. But before we could get far into the subject, one of his hired hands pulled alongside with a tractor to hook up to the Gehl Mix Mill that rested behind me. There is a lot to be said about tractors. But if I had to choose between the smell of hog manure and the smell of diesel exhaust, I would take manure every time. Between the noise and odor, Marvin and I agreed with a look and a nod to get up and walk toward the house.

With the racket receding and the sweet, nutty smell of manure once again filling our noses, Marvin returned to the subject of his contracts. With a dry laugh, he called them "the bane of my existence."

Remember, this is someone who appears to be living the Jeffersonian dream. Marvin again: "I own 1,090 acres and rent another 400, which is more than I owned back when times were good. All the buildings, mine too." At $7,633 per acre, the average price of Iowa farmland in 2016 (though Marvin's land is definitely above average), his landholdings total more than $8.3 million. He has also invested more than $1.5 million in various facilities to raise his hogs.

Wait. Calling them *his* hogs isn't quite right because, technically, they're not.

"From the outside, I could see someone thinking that it's a pretty equitable arrangement. Hell, I thought that way at first." Marvin's contract was structured a lot like the hundreds of others that I have been shown. The farmer supplies all the labor, land, and buildings, "Though," Marvin was quick to add, "the facilities need to be built to very specific specifications, which means they can't be easily repurposed for something else." Meanwhile, the buyer supplies everything else: vet services, feed, transportation, and animals.

Marvin proceeded to tell me about the tens of thousands of dollars' worth of new gestation crates that he was recently required to buy.

Gestation crates, also known as sow stalls, are metal enclosures—Marvin's were roughly six and half feet long by two feet wide—for female breeding pigs. They are usually found only in more intensive hog operations. The expense was made even more difficult to swallow in Marvin's case, as the old crates "worked perfectly fine; they were just too large." He explained that the change was made to "cram more sows into the farrowing barn."

We could debate the welfare implications of this switch, not that I think there is much to debate. Cramming sows into even smaller spaces is a step backward, on multiple levels. This investment also made it exponentially harder for him to rethink his business model, especially if the alternative involved producing something else. You cannot really do much with gestation crates outside of hog production.

As we discussed his contract, an old saying kept coming to mind: the devil lies in the details. And those details in Marvin's case were devilish. In negotiating his contract, Marvin never really had a chance. Processors have their pick of farmers. Meanwhile, farmers are lucky to have more than one buyer to select from. Farmers in these situations lack exit power, the power to walk away from the negotiating table, which means they lack leverage, making them price *takers* rather than negotiators. In Marvin's case, his contract is structured in such a way that he is "getting less" than what he "used to receive back when there were a couple buyers to choose from," like back when he was envied by an eight-year-old for his VHS player and twenty-inch-plus television.

I asked Marvin why he accepted such an arrangement. Having known him for more than thirty-five years, I felt comfortable taking the direct approach. His eyes immediately fixed upon his hands, almost as if he did not want to look me in the eye. Then, sheepishly, he answered, "I know; stupid, right? Yeah, I knew I wasn't going to be making as much. But at least I knew I had a long-term contract. Beggars can't be choosers."

There you have it: market concentration makes beggars out of farmers.

I am not suggesting that processors are bad people. They are taking full advantage of the fact that farmers in these situations need their business. That dependence also increases over time, which was Marvin's point when telling me about how his buildings were "built to very specific specifications, which means they can't be easily repurposed for something else."

Think back to those gestation crates—cages that have trapped Marvin every bit as much as his sows. When you invest $1 million into a facility with a thirty-year life and no practical alternative use, you suddenly have a million new reasons to renew your contract and a million reasons for overlooking how unfairly structured it is.

As if things couldn't get worse . . .

On October 17, 2017, the U.S. Department of Agriculture announced that it was withdrawing the Farmer Fair Practices Rules—or the Grain Inspection, Packers, and Stockyards Administration (GIPSA) rules, as they're more commonly known. The move was essentially the government giving the middle finger to farmers such as Marvin.

Marvin's life would not have changed all that much had the rules been allowed to go into effect. But these Obama-era rules would have made it a little easier for livestock farmers to sue processors or meat-packers over unfair treatment by updating language in the Packers and Stockyards Act of 1921. Farmers currently have little legal recourse to all the unfair treatment described here. Marvin's buyers could tell him to build any sort of structure they want, no matter how outrageous. Noncompliance could be grounds for breach of contract and would certainly jeopardize contract extension.

Right now, and for the foreseeable future—thanks, USDA—Marvin would need to prove "competitive injury" if he wanted to take his buyers to court: a legal bar that would have been lowered considerably had the rule gone into effect. In practical terms, this means he would need to prove that a company's actions against him harmed competition *throughout the entire industry*. This burden of proof is as irrational as it is insurmountable. It is like saying that if punched, you would have to prove that the assault harmed all of society in order to claim punitive damages from your assailant.

Farmers deserve better.

I met Jack during a thunderstorm, which seemed to portend the discussion that followed. Over coffee and cinnamon rolls, and between cracks of thunder, Jack told me a harrowing story.

A few years back, on a night not unlike the one unfolding beyond the dry confines of his house, Jack had heard a knock on his door. Answering it, he discovered two gentlemen. Claiming to be surveying area farmers on behalf of the state's land grant university, they asked him a few questions. (They didn't show credentials, and Jack didn't ask to see them, midwestern hospitality norms being what they are.) The men were interested in the seed he had planted in recent seasons, the herbicides he had used, and where he had taken his crops after harvest. Then, as quickly as they had appeared, the men thanked him for his time and turned back into the rain, never to be seen by Jack again.

It took six days, and some sleuthing on his part, to discover their true identities. Turns out they'd been asking questions around town about him. These visitors were investigators for Monsanto, an agrochemical and agricultural biotechnology company.

Parts of Jack's story sounded like something right out of the Jack Reacher series by Lee Child: clandestine agents lurking in his fields trying to obtain unauthorized seed samples, and Jack, never far from his shotgun while doing chores—purely for intimidation, he assured me. I could not verify that anyone actually trespassed, though I did see two large RedHead gun safes in Jack's machine shed, right next to a reloading bench with a shotgun shell press.

Monsanto does not inspect all the farms using its products. The company's pockets are deep, but not *that* deep. Typically, it works from information gleaned from its tip line. The company strongly encourages farmers to report neighbors they suspect of using its seed unlawfully— generally anytime Monsanto's seed is saved and replanted.

We are talking about seed the farmers bought. Seed that will produce new seed, which farmers will then harvest, with their own sweat and equipment. Seed they will then take to a grain elevator to sell, presumably because it's theirs. Right?

Farmers effectively sign away their ownership rights the moment they buy most commercial seed. Remember what I said earlier about the devil being in the details of contracts. Seed use agreements are devilishly detailed. All farmers using Monsanto's products must sign a Monsanto Technology/Stewardship Agreement, wherein they agree to a list of stipulations. To quote directly from one such agreement dated a few years back, users agree to things such as these:

- "To use Seed containing Monsanto Technologies solely for planting a single commercial crop;
- "Not to save any crop produced from Seed for planting and not to supply Seed produced from Seed to anyone for planting other than to a Monsanto licensed seed company;
- "Not to save or clean any crop produced from Seed for planting and not to supply Seed produced from Seed;
- "Not to transfer any Seed containing patented Monsanto Technologies to any other person or entity for planting;

- "To use on Roundup Ready crops only labeled Roundup agricultural herbicides or other authorized non-selective herbicide which could not be used in the absence of the Roundup Ready gene. [Farmers here are being told what herbicide to use. No surprise; it's owned by Monsanto too.]
- "To allow Monsanto to examine and copy any records and receipts that could be relevant to Grower's performance of this Agreement."

Note the openness of this language: records and receipts that *could* be relevant to the agreement. This essentially gives Monsanto access to any and all paperwork linked to a farmer's business.

There is one additional stipulation in the agreement worth highlighting. Located in the section titled "Grower Receives from Monsanto Company," farmers are said to receive "a limited use license to purchase and plant seed containing Monsanto Technologies ('Seed') and apply Roundup agricultural herbicides and other authorized non-selective herbicides over the top of Roundup Ready crops."

Jack swore that he did not violate any of the agreement's terms. And yet, he settled out of court. When asked why, all he could initially muster, a whole octave higher than his normal speaking voice, was, "*Me* take on *Monsanto*—are you nuts?" What the actual terms of his settlement were, he would not say. Settling sealed his secrecy on the specifics, thanks to a nondisclosure agreement written by Monsanto attorneys.

You might think such an experience would have given Jack pause, enough even to change management practices, maybe even occupations. You might think that, if you didn't understand farmers. It is easy to confuse stubbornness with pride, inflexibility, and independence. It is not being stubborn to protect one's own house, family, and lifestyle. Wars have been based on less than that.

Jack also admitted to farming pretty much as he always has, minus the Monsanto products. Whether it is his choice to stay the course is a matter for debate.

I asked him directly how he might change his operation if he could. Just then, a loud clap of thunder sent our backs upright. Our muscles loosened as the sound waned, rolling off into the distance.

Jack resumed looking into his coffee as though there weren't a question left unanswered. I knew he was thinking, so I amused myself by surveying the collection of U.S. President plates displayed in a nearby hutch.

Still staring into his mug, Jack continued: "There are days when I think about changing how I farm. But let's get real. I've got loans to pay off, landlords too. I can't grow anything I want, not without a market. And I'm just one guy, so I don't exactly have leverage to shape markets. My hands are tied."

Our interview concluded in typical fashion, with me asking if he would like to add anything. He blew out air through his mouth, scrubbed a hand across his face, and then took a deep breath, through his nose this time.

"You would think I'm in control of my destiny. I have land and buildings, good ground, lots of good equipment. My debt is a fraction of what some of the guys around me are grappling with."

I wasn't quite sure what Jack was building toward, but at this point he looked up and ran both hands through his hair, from front to back. Only then did I notice how bloodshot his eyes were. They hadn't been like that earlier. The man before me was clearly frustrated.

"There are times I regret having it all. Having all this can feel more like a burden when it should be freeing. How f*cked up is that?"

Jeb is a corn, soybean, and wheat farmer living in central Nebraska. Now in his mid-forties, he has lived his whole life in the same house, save for the four years when he was getting his degree in agricultural economics at the University of Nebraska. I was visiting the state to learn more about its proposed Fair Repair Act, which was introduced into the Nebraska legislature in January 2016. Some farmers are trying to reclaim the right to fix their own equipment. Not a wild proposition, as this population includes the original do-it-yourselfers. As for folks like Jeb—farmer by day, right-to-repair activist by night—they are leading the charge to reclaim that right.

It's funny—sad funny, not ha-ha funny—how agriculture went from being an inoculant from dependence to a path into it. We have already seen how structural changes to markets have made farmers dependent on processors. The Fair Repair Act looks to tackle a different type of dependence, specifically farmers' reliance on dealers and other approved technicians to keep their equipment running.

The federal Digital Millennium Copyright Act of 1998 (DMCA), passed to prevent digital piracy, is a key piece of legislation in this story. It effectively made it illegal for equipment owners to access the software that runs their equipment. In practical terms, it meant that after 1998, farmers must have implement dealers perform work in which the equipment's engine control unit is accessed. As there are few repairs that can be done on farm equipment that do not also require cracking into its computer, the resulting dependence has created yet another reliable revenue stream for farm implement firms.

There are practical reasons for wanting to be able to fix your own equipment or to have the option of having someone other than an "approved" technician do it. As Jeb explained, "Sometimes there's nothing mechanically wrong with the equipment. Something gets tripped and the entire system shuts down and needs to be reset. So I lose two days of work and a couple hundred bucks to have some guy come out and hit a few buttons."

He proceeded to tell me about when the transmission went out in one of his tractors. His neighbor, Nick, is a diesel and transmission mechanic and "a hell of a guy," Jeb assured me. As he had done dozens of times before, he looked to Nick to be his repairman. No harm, no foul, according to federal copyright legislation. While John Deere would have undoubtedly preferred that he have his equipment repaired at one of its dealerships, there was not much it could do. The tractor was no longer under warranty. And we're talking about a transmission repair, not a software upgrade.

"But then," Jeb said, "we got the transmission installed." I looked up at him, expecting him to say more. His eyes met mine and he winked. Or perhaps it was a tic, as it was almost indiscernible and he was clearly agitated. His cool blue eyes looking more through me than at me, he explained how he "still needed those SOBs after all to get it back to my yard."

Turns out the part still had to be authorized by an approved service provider, which would allow the computer to *recognize* the part. No recognize, no go. Jeb shelled out $230 plus $130 per hour to get someone from the nearest implement dealership, fifty miles away, to, as he put it, "plug in a computer and hit the 'authorize' button."

That's not the worst of it. The most important input of all in agriculture is time. More than money, these repairs cost farmers their least renewable resource—the one thing they can't grow, any more than they can borrow it from a bank. Jeb again: "Even if I have a legitimate repair, you've got to understand farming is all about timing. If rain is coming and I need to get a crop in or out, that means I need to get out there ASAP, to say nothing of the fact that we're always chasing daylight, especially in the fall, when darkness comes far too early." Farmers generally are not comfortable placing the success or failure of their enterprise in the hands of someone else, which is what it feels like when they have field work to do but are waiting for the next available technician.

Earlier in this chapter, I mentioned the devilish details of contract farming and Monsanto's user agreements. Here's another, this time concerning the contracts John Deere has crafted for farmers who "buy" its equipment. The contracts stipulate that the company cannot be sued in the event that farmers lose money because repair delays prevent them from tending to their crops.

Concerning the legal question of ownership, John Deere made the argument in 2015 to the U.S. Copyright Office that farmers receive "an implied license for the life of the vehicle to operate the vehicle."[3] In some respects, the company was taking a cue from Monsanto's gene and seed owning playbook, saying farmers were buying a license and not an actual thing. The reason for the memo was that an exemption to the DMCA was being considered and John Deere wished for a continuation of the status quo. Later that year, in October, a decision was made that surprised many. The Librarian of Congress ruled in favor of the exemption, allowing anyone who owned a tractor—or car, truck, or other vehicle—to tinker with its code. (The Librarian of Congress holds a curious position. He or she oversees the operation of the world's largest library, with a staff that numbers in the thousands and a collection in the millions, in addition to the U.S. Copyright Office, the government office that manages the registration of all copyrighted materials.)

Shortly after the ruling, *Forbes* published an article titled "DMCA Ruling Ensures You Can't Be Sued for Hacking Your Car, Your Games, or Your iPhone."[4] Chalk one up for the little guy. Right? No so fast. The matter, I'm afraid, is more complex than that.

Around the time that the exemption was granted, John Deere started requiring farmers to sign a licensing agreement. The agreement sought to undo the actions of the United States' top librarian by expressly forbidding nearly all personal repairs and modifications to farming equipment, directing owners to dealerships and authorized repair shops.

The document is the same one that also prevents farmers from suing for "crop loss, damage to land, damage to machines, lost profits, loss of business or loss of goodwill, loss of use of equipment . . . arising from the performance or non-performance of any aspect of the software."[5]

Not that they really needed to do that.

For one thing, the exemption extends only to the individual who purchased the equipment. Only the owner has the authority to access and fiddle with the tractor's software. The moment she brings her nonapproved technician to look at it, she crosses a legal line in the sand, and they both become liable for copyright infringement. A grayer area involves the question of what level of tinkering by an owner is allowed under the exemption. According to attorneys knowledgeable on the subject, the exemption allows for only certain repairs, which is why I have been using the term "tinkering." For example, software platforms connected to operator safety and vehicle emissions, because of the fact that agencies with nothing to do with copyright law oversee their regulation and compliance, cannot be touched. Just ask Volkswagen, which got caught with its hand in *that* cookie jar. Tampering with software to circumvent emissions regulations got the company slapped with $4.3 billion in fines in 2015.

Through interviews with right-to-repair activists—or hacktivists, as some liked to be called—I also learned about a burgeoning online market for pirated John Deere software from Poland and Ukraine. Examples include John Deere Service Advisor, which allows farmers to recalibrate tractors and diagnose broken parts; John Deere PayLoad files, which allow farmers to customize and fine-tune elements of their equipment from the chassis, engine, and cab; and John Deere Electronic Data Link drivers, which are needed for one's computer to communicate with the tractor's hardware.

Jeb admitted to knowing some people who had tried this black market equipment, quickly assuring me that he never did anything that could get him in trouble with John Deere. When he said this, he gave me a wink—and this time it was definitely a wink.

Back to Nebraska's proposed Fair Repair Act. The exemption also requires renewal every year. The Fair Repair Act would make the exemption permanent. The bill also "requests"—not the strongest legal language—that operating manuals and diagnostic equipment be made available to farmers. It is hard to fix anything if you do not have access to the necessary materials to troubleshoot and eventually pinpoint what is in need of repair.

Near the end of our interview, Jeb took me into his machine shed. We had been talking about the value of diagnostic equipment, and he had mentioned that he wanted to show me something. Walking in, I noticed immediately layered odors drifting in the air: the low smell of cats and hay, coupled with the higher, acrid sting that could only have been fertilizer, and, sandwiched between, the cool scent of fall air blowing in through the oversized door. Standing there, taking in the enormity of the space, I watched Jeb walk over to a workbench. He grabbed a small device that looked like a stud finder. "Today's tractors"—he tipped his head in the direction of the John Deere 6210R resting ten yards to my right—"aren't really any more difficult to fix than the ones I grew up fixing when I was a kid in the 1970s." Holding the code reader at chest level, he told me, "Until software and diagnostic equipment are available, and until people can put that equipment to work on their smart tractors, farmers will continue to be under the thumb of large implement firms."

Jeb and others presented me with a scenario that usually came up in discussions of how corporations aggressively assert their property rights over those of farmers. As Jeb put the question, "What would happen if John Deere suddenly decided to stop servicing its equipment?" I doubt strongly that this will ever happen. But it raises an important point, namely, that until farmers have true ownership of their farm equipment, they cannot even learn how to make those repairs. Which makes that scenario a scary one, no matter how unlikely.

Jeb used this memorable analogy when describing the risk: "It's like relying on someone else to breathe for you; if I couldn't get my equipment serviced, my business would suffocate to death."

Here's to making sure that the status quo does not choke off our nation's farmers.

As I stepped through the restaurant's door, the sounds and smells hit me all at once. The espresso machine was whizzing and whining, cutting through the steady murmur of about a dozen conversations, which inexplicably seemed to crescendo whenever I spoke with the waitress. The scent of bacon and eggs wafted through the air, as did cologne from the businessman seated in the booth behind me and stale musk from the air vent above my head that grew heavier whenever the air conditioner kicked in. Just your typical morning at Faye's Place.

My meeting with Faye—*the* Faye—almost never happened. She was twenty minutes late for the interview. With my coffee and breakfast finished, I began feeling guilty about holding the table. When she came out from her office, she immediately apologized. "I was stuck on the phone with a lender. Trying to get another merchant cash advance. You familiar with those? Argh, I hate making those phone calls!"

In hindsight, I consider myself lucky that she was delayed. My plan had not been to talk with her about merchant cash advances. I did not even know what they were at the time.

Merchant cash advances are advertised, aggressively in some cases, to small businesses as fast cash. Since the recession a decade ago, credit has dried up for all but the largest businesses. Many upstart entrepreneurs would be happy to have access to *any* cash. That it is *fast* is an added bonus.

But fast isn't all it's cut out to be. The phrase "pulling a fast one" comes to mind when talking to someone on the receiving end of these loans.

The process works something like this. A loan is made to a business owner, taken out as an advance on future sales. The lender then makes automatic deductions from daily credit or debit card sales or by regularly deducting money from the business's bank account. The loan also comes with a hefty interest rate.

In Faye's case, she was given an advance of roughly $20,000. Just to get the loan, she was assessed close to $1,000 in processing fees. The lender then deducted more than $400 per day from her business's sales for seventy days. With fees, Faye paid back slightly less than $30,000, on a loan for $20,000 that lasted a little over two months. That is an effective interest rate in the *triple* digits.

Faye is also African American. I mention that because credit is even harder to come by for black and Latino business owners. One recent study looked at nine businessmen—three white, three black, and three Hispanic.[6] Similar in size, age, and gender, wearing the same outfits and claiming identical education levels and financial profiles, they visited different banks seeking a $60,000 loan to grow identical businesses. And yet, their experiences once inside were very different. Compared with their white counterparts, the minority small-business owners were given less information about loan terms, were asked more questions about their personal finances, and were offered less assistance by loan officers.

Faye again, describing past conversations with neighbors and fellow business owners: "I can tell you that people owning businesses in this neighborhood are targeted—phone calls, mailings, whatever it takes—by these lenders." Faye's café is in a minority-majority community—more nonwhites than whites. She continued by comparing these experiences with those described by friends who own businesses "out by the mall," in an affluent and largely white community. "Most don't even know what a merchant advance loan is. That's no coincidence."

We ended the interview in her office. The pretense was that she wanted to show me a photo of when President Obama had visited her café. But I also got the sense that our conversation had taken a nerve touching turn and that she wanted some privacy, away from our somewhat nosy waitress—she liked to hover. Once we were inside, Faye's demeanor changed. It soon became clear she was managing her emotions more in the prior public space than I had realized.

"I got into all this because I wanted to be my own boss. Turns out I'm the one being bossed around. I want to do so much—pay my workers a decent wage; make fresh, healthy, inexpensive food for a community that doesn't have it; donate food to community projects." Her restaurant is located in a USDA recognized food desert. Faye then reached for a tissue from a box sitting on her desk, folded it, and dabbed the corner of her left eye. Tears.

Looking down at the tissue, now balled up in her hand, she said, "I just wish there were another way, where I could be a small-business owner without all the headache and heartburn, where I'd be able to take *actual* ownership of my business."

For all the Fayes in the world: this book recognizes the burdens of ownership, which include the burdens brought on by financing the Jeffersonian ideal.

CHAPTER 2
When Sharing Is Illegal

Noelle is a labor attorney. Two decades of helping corporations skirt labor laws—*lawfully* skirt, she assured me—had taken its toll. "Got to the point where I couldn't take it anymore," she confided. "I wasn't making the world any better; I certainly wasn't helping my fellow man. My job was to enrich companies, even if that meant pulling the rug out from under hardworking families." She did not want to disclose what rugs precisely she pulled. She is an attorney, let's not forget—a population that knows better than most how not to self-incriminate. Whatever happened had led her down a road to starting her own practice. Her days are now devoted to, in her own words, "helping people share."

One unexpected thing to come out of my journey in understanding the sharing economy was to learn about the *legal* impediments to collaboration resulting from existing labor laws. It is ironic in some ways. The very laws designed to reduce the blunt force trauma created by the ownership economy are keeping us from truly enacting something new and different. This might sound harsh, but the current system does a pretty good job of incentivizing exploitation. When you make more money by treating people poorly—by paying them less, skirting labor laws, refusing to provide adequate health care, and so forth—is that not the definition of incentivizing bad behavior? So we *should* have strong labor laws: rules to ensure that employers pay their employees, and pay them at least a minimum wage, like what we have under the Fair Labor Standards Act.[1] Unfortunately, the laws we have in place, while well intentioned, are ill advised, especially if we hope to kick off a collaborative revolution.

Noelle's office was next to an elementary school, and our conversation was punctuated by the occasional prepubescent scream. This, coupled with her relaxed, forthright demeanor, gave the interview a laid-back feel. I remember wondering if a nonsharing attorney would be as giving of his or her time and expertise.

We talked first about how current laws are too rigid. As most are currently written or interpreted, all individuals laboring for the material benefit of others, even when it is *shared*, can be lumped into the "employee" category.[2] Whether the act is motivated by love, reciprocal commitments, kinship ties, or altruism is irrelevant.[3] Noelle reminded me that the rationale is perfectly admirable, especially when applied to the ownership economy, namely, to ensure that no one slips through the cracks. As she put it, "I would never want a system in place where employers have the ability to cajole prospective employees into signing away their rights. So we've historically sought labor laws with those worst-case scenarios in mind."

Bells outside started ringing. Like air being let out of a balloon, kids began to stream out of a large double door and onto the playground, creating a crescendo as more left the building for recess. After closing the window, Noelle noted that assuming the worst of employers "doesn't accurately depict relationships in a more collaborative-type economy." In the dog-eat-dog world to which existing labor laws are directed, employer and employee are by definition not the same person. Not so under more collaborative business arrangements.

My meeting with Noelle was pivotal on a few levels. I walked into her office thinking the biggest legal challenges faced by the sharing economy revolved around property law, including intellectual property law. Naïvely, I did not have labor law on my radar, but I walked out with a newfound appreciation for questions about labor. Not only that, my meeting with Noelle brought with it a renewed faith in labor attorneys—strike that: *sharing economy* labor attorneys.

I also have Noelle to thank for connecting me with a variety of individuals who had wanted to grow the sharing economy only to discover they legally could not—people like Marcus, a bear of a man with a laugh befitting a person of his stature.

"The story was a major wake-up call for the industry," he told me shortly after our introductory pleasantries. Marcus is the owner of a small winery near Walla Walla, Washington. The story Marcus was referring to came out of Castro Valley, California. Westover Winery had been fined $115,000 by the State of California after it was discovered that the owners were using volunteers for crushing and bottling—not an unusual practice for smaller wineries, I have learned. One volunteer slipped and fell, breaking her arm. The winery did not have workers' compensation insurance, or sufficient business insurance, to cover her injury. The fine was for (1) not paying minimum wage, (2) not providing wage statements, and (3) not paying into workers' compensation insurance.

Marcus confirmed the widespread use of volunteer work in his community. "It's what we do. It's what we've always done, going back a hundred years if you look at how labor was organized in orchards and farms throughout the state." It is no secret how farmers a century ago pooled their labor during harvest. If they had been fined for this practice, it would have killed the agricultural sector and everyone connected to it. I confess to not initially believing Marcus's claim that the practice remains widespread among smaller-scale wineries. Then I took a very nonscientific survey of Facebook pages of wineries in Washington State,

Oregon, and California: more than a dozen shared posts requesting volunteers during crush season.

Washington State leaves small businesses with a little more wiggle room on these matters than California does. The Washington State Department of Labor and Industries provides narrow exemptions under which volunteers can be used. A business needs to have documentation that both parties were aware of the volunteer status prior to work being done. No material compensation can be offered to the volunteer beyond maintenance and reimbursement expenses. This means food can be provided during the event. A bottle of wine is also probably okay, as an expression of gratitude. Finally, the business needs to show that the volunteer work is equally advantageous to both parties. Is the work fun? Does it help build community?

"This isn't about cutting corners. And the thought that we're exploiting our volunteers is outrageous. You talk to any of those who help and they'll make it clear, they *want* to be here," Marcus told me. With that, he got up from behind his desk and walked toward the door. I confess to being seized by fear at that point. Had I offended him by talking about this? Is the interview over? Nope. He stopped at the wall behind me, next to the door, and plucked off a picture. "Look," he instructed, while handing me a framed photo. At the top were the words "Pre Crush Party, 2014." "We need their help to survive." Back behind his desk, he added, "But it's bigger than that. From an economic standpoint, I reinvest a bigger proportion of our revenue into the local community than do the E. and J. Gallos of the world," referring to the Ernest & Julio Gallo Winery, the largest exporter of California wines.

Marcus slapped his knees with both hands, the noise like a dull clap of thunder, and let out one of those larger-than-life laughs. "We're a kinky group. These volunteer parties are important because they *physically*"— he interlocked his hands as though praying—"bring people together."

Common and civil law are suspicious of volunteer labor because it represents, in the words of the U.S. Supreme Court, an "unfair method of competition."[4] Being allowed to use volunteer labor, the argument goes, gives operations an unfair advantage over those that are required to pay their workers and provide benefits, such as workers' compensation insurance. A one-size-fits-all application of employment laws is thus about creating a level playing field. And so: no volunteers, *period.*

If only that logic were applied evenly. The courts cannot possibly think the system they are protecting is fair. Can they?

To take one particularly egregious example: agricultural subsidies. Between 1995 and 2014, the U.S. government paid out $322.7 billion in farm payments. Of this, 75 percent—or $242 billion—went to 10 percent of farms. The average annual payment per recipient among this top 10 percent: $498,442. The tippy-top recipient: Riceland Foods, located in Stuttgart, Arkansas. Between 1995 and 2014, this company— the world's largest miller and marketer of rice, according to its website— received more than half a billion dollars.[5] This single company received more taxpayer monies than did all the farmers in Alaska, Connecticut, Hawaii, Maine, Massachusetts, Nevada, New Hampshire, New Jersey, and Rhode Island *combined.* Is that a fair playing field?

The line between an unfair competitive advantage and an incentive is thin, arbitrary even. To tweak Upton Sinclair's well-worn line about vested interests, it is an "incentive" when your salary depends on it being so. When Walmart enters a community and is given millions in tax incentives, it is called "stimulating the economy." When a small business looks to enter the same marketplace using the free labor of those taxpayers, it is an unfair competitive advantage.

"What we're doing isn't exploitive; it's generative." Now in his bottling facility, Marcus was showing me his mechanical corker and six-bottle-capacity filler—this really was a small-scale operation. "We can't survive if the game is won or lost according to economies of scale, where bigger is better," he told me while demonstrating the corker, adding, "Our survival rests in building connections, community."

Growing a generative, dynamic marketplace: should not that be the goal of economies? Which model would you suppose generates more value: a market dominated by exploitive market concentration or one enriched by collaborative markets? Those I talked with while researching for this book had strong opinions about this. Not surprisingly, all leaned unequivocally toward the latter option.

What look to be highly dynamic and generative business models and what is allowed under the law are misaligned. Marcus again: "I'd love to be able to open my winery up and make it truly community supported, where members could be co-owners and work in exchange for wine and the comradery." Knowing that farm wages where labor intensive crops are grown make up anywhere between 40 and 80 percent of all costs (the higher figure supposes a farm providing livable wages), I can understand Marcus's attraction to this vision, from both community building and strictly financial standpoints.

This is not to deny the fact that people need to make money. We are many miles—heck, a better unit of distance would be astronomical units—away from envisioning a system in which money does not matter. Marcus was not suggesting we replace one one-size-fits-all economy (individual ownership) with another (sharing). In fact, his position is just the opposite. He was looking for the option to scale out instead of only up, where getting *together* is just as acceptable as getting big.

What is wrong with that?

The following legal artifacts—one, a ruling; the other, a statute—were referenced more than once in my conversations with members of a consumer co-op in New York City:

- In *Bobilin v. Board of Education, State of Hawaii* (1975), the court ruled on the question of whether children are employees of a school when doing community service in a cafeteria. The court determined they are not, pointing to "the widespread and common practice of requiring elementary school children to perform small tasks such as erasing blackboards, putting their chairs on their desks after school, and serving as crosswalk monitors." Noting that while these tasks "admittedly do have economic value to the state in that they save the cost of hiring adults to perform these same tasks," they also teach "neatness and responsibility" in addition to "civic attitudes fundamental in a collective society where a citizen is often called upon to 'do his share' without economic compensation." Therefore, "the nature of the service performed by plaintiffs is not 'employment' within the meaning of the FLSA [Fair Labor Standards Act]."[6]
- A Hawaii law (Haw. Rev. Stat. Ann. § 421C-33) makes it legal for people to volunteer for up to twenty-five hours per month when they are a "member of an association." Unfortunately, some sharing economy attorneys believe the statute conflicts with federal employment laws.[7]

Why did co-op members in New York care about laws from a state almost five thousand miles away? Three words: "member worker programs."

Joy and I met in a coffee shop that had plush oversized booths, brownish walls, and glittery beaded curtains. She was clearly a regular, greeting others in the shop by name. An urban gardener, practicing attorney, and self-described community activist, Joy had been recommended to me by two people associated with the New York City cooperative. When I asked her about the legality of member worker programs, it took her a while to get to an answer. As an interviewee, she was a bit like a pitcher with no one on base. There was no avoiding the windup.

"Co-ops around the country are founded on this tradition, either where members can choose to work for a larger discount or where all are required to work. It's about access, community solidarity, and economic survival." Joy had been with the cooperative since it was founded, in the 1970s. While explaining what she meant by "access" and "economic survival," she made the claim that her co-op had "the least expensive food in town." As I teach my students when encountering unexpected claims made during field research, trust, but verify. So I did. Price-checking a sample basket of grocery items from a nearby Fairway Market confirmed Joy's assertion. The co-op basket: $74.91. Fairway's identical basket: $99.88—a 25 percent costlier shopping trip.

The member worker program, by keeping labor costs low and member commitment high, has demonstrable benefits for the co-op and its members. Yet some want to do away with it.

Certain members, according to Joy, were worried that the co-op might be violating minimum wage laws and worker compensation requirements. The more I learned about the debate, which played out in meetings and in the members-only portion of the co-op's website, the more tangled it became. Civil law, specifically the Fair Labor Standards Act, is pretty expansive in its understanding of who is an employee. Whether or not a worker is an employee, in the eyes of the FLSA, hinges on this bit of legalese: an employee is "any individual employed by an employer."[8]

Yet a scan of common law—law established through court precedent—will reveal numerous rulings giving the member worker program cover, such as the Hawaiian court case mentioned earlier. Joy was also the first to tell me about the aforementioned law legalizing volunteer work for up to twenty-five hours per month, explaining how it needs to be enacted at the federal level. "As an attorney, you get used to working in the art of interpreting law. But this area, especially around member worker programs, is particularly gray, which is why we need something like that from Congress"—the "that" referred to being Haw. Rev. Stat. Ann. § 421C-33.

I later learned from another individual with the cooperative that members in the 1980s asked the state's department of labor for advice on the subject and were told that member workers were entitled to a minimum wage. That ought to have put an end to the practice, according to some. Upon hearing that piece of information, I initially leaned in that direction, too. Then I talked to Lyle.

Lyle was recently retired from the New York State Department of Labor, which might account for his candor. Talking about member worker programs, Lyle admitted that the department had been asked by cooperatives over the years to give legal advice. He was refreshingly frank about how regulatory agencies, in his opinion, approach these queries. "Generally, we have a practice of wanting to err on the side of caution. The last thing we want is to say a practice is legal, have it challenged in the courts, and have our opinions proven wrong."

The entire incentive structure seems to be working against sharing, from laws that criminalize "employers" who enlist volunteers, even when volunteers are employers and vice versa (e.g., in cooperatives), to policing authorities who explicitly "err on the side of caution" for fear of being proven wrong by the courts. Lyle spoke of a disconnect between "the world envisioned by proponents of sharing economies and today's laws, which were designed primarily to protect us from markets premised more on hostility than reciprocity." His comment echoes a point made earlier: conventional labor laws assume the worst of businesses, making it hard for those who want to do something socially positive.

We wrapped up our conversation by talking about the future of the sharing economy and the barriers that still stand in its way. For Lyle, change must happen at the top: "Until Congress recognizes sharing, labor laws as they apply to things like volunteering will forever remain subject to political winds."

All the more reason for building bridges rather than fences: the answer to *how* this political pressure is going to grow. While I agree with Lyle that change has to take place at the top, it is not going to start there. We have to force the hands of our elected officials on this one. Only by working together can we hope to design laws that encourage sharing while still protecting workers.

The same rules for everyone. Sounds reasonable—right?

I had been reading for some time about the plight of small-scale Southeast Asian family farmers—predominantly Hmong, Iu Mien, and Lao refugees—in California's Central Valley. The stories have similarities. There is always an extended family with a compelling immigration tale of leaving poverty and oppression behind for a slice of the American dream. Eventually, the dream turns into a nightmare. The boogeyman is often a government official, an inspector, typically. In a case of the pen being scarier than the sword, the household finds itself facing onerous fines for any number of infractions. Those violations include anything from using the labor of minors (their own children, grandchildren, nieces, and nephews, mind you) to not paying minimum wage, not carrying workers' compensation insurance, failing to provide gender segregated toilets, not having a Cal/OSHA approved Injury and Illness Prevention Program (Cal/OSHA is the state's Division of Occupational Safety and Health), failing to put a Not Potable Water sign at the designated handwashing station, not having all the right posters (yes, *posters*) carrying various regulatory messages, and not providing single-use water cups. After years of reading others' accounts, I decided it was time to go to the source.

When Dawb greeted me at the door, I noticed immediately the center stone in her necklace. A large black onyx gemstone: beautifully cut and polished, it seemed to draw all the light in the entryway toward it. She fiddled nervously with it as she invited me out to her garden.

Stepping off the porch, she told me a bit about her family's history. Dawb's mother and father had moved to California when she was just a child, from the mountainous region of China just north of the Vietnam border. She also made a brief reference to "political persecution," reaching for that gemstone again, this time with both hands. I got the sense that she did not want to dredge up the past. That was not why I was there anyway, so I stuck to questions about her farm.

Dawb's family farmed a little over five acres. About half of the produce went to feeding the household; the surplus was sold at a roadside stand and to a few restaurants. That's how they got themselves into trouble. That last bit, without requisite practices in place, was a no-no in the eyes of the law.

Let's be clear: we are not talking about sales that generated a lot of money. In fact, they added up to below minimum wage for the adults involved.

Two weeks prior, not far from the very bench on which we were sitting, an official from the state's Division of Labor Standards Enforcement had cited Dawb. Her offenses, among other things, included not having workers' compensation insurance and not paying her non-nuclear family members a wage. The total penalty exceeded $10,000, close to an entire year's profits for the household. She admitted that she didn't know what her family would do in future seasons. And as that future is now upon us, I'm afraid to ask, for fear of self-incrimination.

After she told me this story, we just sat there. I remember staring at a patch of lemongrass as I wondered what to ask next. Dawb's voice broke through the awkward silence as she told me about her experience of looking into workers' compensation insurance. It was an excellent example of laws written without enterprises like hers in mind.

Dawb had discovered not only that insurance policies are pricey but also that their term length makes them cost prohibitive. Trying to stifle the pain in her voice, she said, "We can't get a policy for less than three months." She turned her head in my direction but looked through me, adding, "Those policies don't work when you're dealing with planting and harvest seasons that run only a week or two in the spring and again in the fall."

Dawb's case is an important reminder that evenly applied laws alone do not a robust and just collaborative economy make. Take translation services, or lack thereof. Among these Hmong, Iu Mien, and Lao households, most adults speak limited English, while they might be inspected by people who speak only English. People are being fined without even understanding why.

This is all to say that worker regulations can hurt as well as protect people, and we need to learn the difference.

Marcie had lived in the Bay Area her entire life, all sixty-five years of it. Forty-five of those were spent in the restaurant industry in and around San Francisco, as a short-order cook, baker, head chef, sommelier, and, just prior to retiring, general manager. She left that world to take care of her ailing husband. Not long after doing that, she saw an ad for Josephine, an online platform promising to help home cooks coordinate their small-scale takeout business. "Wanted: Outgoing people who love to cook and who are good at it. The shy and those who hate to cook need not apply!" The business model is fairly straightforward. (In February 2018, executives of this Oakland-based start-up announced the imminent closure of the business after almost four years, following a series of legal ups and downs.)[9] Those who sign up make meals in their home and then post them online. After placing an order, the buyer picks the food up at a prearranged time. The chef gets 90 percent of the revenue; Josephine gets the rest.

"I knew I needed to be at home, but I couldn't give up food," Marcie explained. "Josephine gave me something to do that was for me." I learned about Marcie's business from a friend and frequent customer of her crawfish and shrimp gumbo. This friend was born and raised in southern Louisiana, so to hear her describe the dish as "out of this world" says something about Marcie's culinary skills.

I first talked to Marcie about two weeks before taking a trip to California. My plan was to meet her in person and hear more about her thriving business. I was also looking forward to talking to whoever happened to drop by her house to pick up food. The day prior to my flight, I received the following cryptic e-mail message from her: "Got shut down. Cease and desist order. Come out if you want. Still happy to talk but can't promise dry eyes." Twelve hundred miles later, I was sitting at Marcie's kitchen table. She handed me the order. "I was told I was committing a misdemeanor, punishable by jail if I didn't stop. Just for cooking food in my own kitchen!" Marcie was clearly pained, her eyes glistening as she pounded her chest with two clenched fists in tempo with the words "my own kitchen."

Not long after my trip to California, District Judge Vince Girdhari Chhabria of the U.S. District Court for the Northern District of California likened the sharing economy to a square peg and existing laws to round holes.[10] Later in the same decision, he opined about how twentieth-century law "isn't very helpful in addressing this"—"this" being the growing number of legal questions surrounding the sharing economy—a "21st Century problem."[11]

The health department officials who stopped Marcie from continuing her trade chose one such hole, treating her business like any other commercial enterprise. That particular hole leads to very clear lines of questioning: had Marcie's kitchen been inspected and certified, and did it have all the necessities as dictated by law? Triple sink: wash, rinse, and sanitize?—no comingling! Grease trap? Dedicated washroom for employees? Commercial refrigeration? HACCP (Hazard Analysis

Critical Control Points) food safety management systems? Crack-free floors? Lighting fixtures with nonbreakable lenses?

That hole, if the city really wanted to play hardball, could have also resulted in Marcie being cited for noncompliance with the Americans with Disabilities Act (ADA). To pick up their food, neighbors were required to hurdle two separate sets of stairs. One regular customer had, in Marcie's words, "mobility issues." Marcie simply walked his order out to his car, as he could park directly in front of her house—problem solved, from the standpoint of all parties concerned. The government, however, might not have seen it that way, if it had bothered to look.

Another round hole casts Marcie's cooking simply as the activities of a private individual.[12] This is how Marcie saw things, and how the majority of those engaged in the sharing economy view these practices, as perfectly legal and even worthy of tax-exempt status. They're private transactions, after all, or so folks like Marcie say. (The Internal Revenue Service, not surprisingly, holds a different opinion.)[13] According to this line of thought, people around the country prepare food for others all the time and avoid the scrutiny of overzealous food police. Sure, Marcie sold food she prepared. But is that qualitatively different from selling your baked goods at a local church's bake sale? What about those quid pro quo food exchanges between neighbors, in which those with gardens give friends buckets of fresh fruits and vegetables, receiving in return any number of items or services?

Let us not forget that when sociologist Marcel Mauss set out to study socially enabled exchanges nearly a century ago, he found gift relations to be even *more* indebting than money based exchanges in some ways.[14] This is not to suggest that altruism does not exist, just that we can feel indebted in many ways and that *monetary* indebtedness and *social* indebtedness are more similar than we might wish to admit.

I recall telling Marcie jokingly—*jokingly*, for any health department officials out there—that she should restart her business, this time giving customers a quick palm reading when they pick up their food and charging for that instead of for the food. Some chefs actually do things like this to exploit loopholes and to give their square peg the appearance of being round. I recently visited a pop-up restaurant that operated this way; attendees were instructed to pay for the live music while receiving "complimentary" food.

You will not hear me arguing on behalf of this hole—or any hole: remember, we're dealing with square pegs. Just as I want laws that enable sharing, I do not want to make it easier for unscrupulous people to act unscrupulously. In other words, sharing should not be a Trojan horse for deregulation. Why this reluctance to embrace the private citizen hole? One big reason: private individuals can legally discriminate. You can choose, for instance, whom you invite into your home for your son's parties, dinner, a barbecue, you name it. And if you wish to have over only whites, or Christians, Muslims, Native Americans, Chicago Cubs fans, close talkers, or vegans—whomever—you are well within your rights to do so. After all, it's your home.

That's not sharing. It's bigotry.

CHAPTER 3

The Promise of Access

Land succession: here is a topic that you will be reading and hearing more about in the years ahead.

Demographic realities, such as the fact that the average age among U.S. farmers is approaching sixty, are expected to result in some 70 percent of the nation's farmland changing hands in the next twenty years.[1] As an official of the U.S. Department of Agriculture recently told me, "We're ten years away from the largest land transfer in the history of the country."

Authors overuse the "crossroads" metaphor, but in this case, the term is apt. More than 600 million of the 900 million acres currently in production are expected to change hands in the next couple of decades.[2] Individuals who identify as white own 98 percent of all farmland nationally.[3] Farmland ownership patterns might change, radically even, perhaps in ways that better represent the country's demography. Or not: a survey of California landowners revealed that 79 percent of respondents planned to place their parcels permanently into family or individual trusts.[4] If that is not a crossroads, I do not know what you would call it.

Farmland inflation rates in the United States have increased by roughly 150 percent in the past fifteen years, propelling the price of ground in some states above $13,000 per acre.[5] Rising commodity prices have a role to play in this.[6] Another factor is government subsidies, which cause farmers to become less risk averse.[7] If you know the government is standing by with a safety net, whether through subsidized crop insurance or price supports, you are likely going to be willing to pay more for land when it becomes available.

Farmland inflation has also made the rich richer.[8] Landowners reinvest their growing assets by buying more equipment and yet more land—which accounts for a staggering 85 percent of farm assets in the United States.[9] The landed haves, in other words, become the landed *have mores*. And more. And more.

Talk to any farmer or aspiring one. Ninety-nine out of one hundred will say there is really only one alternative to owning land: renting. Approximately 45 percent of all farmland—that's close to 400 million acres—in the United States is rented.

The reality is that rented land tends to be leased to individuals who already farm, with added priority given to large-scale operations. Landlords generally have no interest in overseeing hundreds of accounts. Who would? We're talking mostly about retirees here, hardworking folk who are looking to enjoy spending time with their grandchildren, not hunched over computers plugging entries into their financial software as they try to manage dozens of small leases. It is a lot easier to rent ground by the *hundreds* of acres, which is far more land than what's needed by beginning farmers looking to supply local and regional markets.

Tom, the USDA official earlier quoted, explained why tenant farming supports more of the same. "Most landlords are retirees using their land as a 401(k), using it to finance their retirement. They want to keep it simple by leasing their land to one person, or to two at the most." He took out his pocketknife and proceeded to scrape his cuticles. Looking at his fingers, he added, "Since this is their retirement, they want to rent to a known entity, meaning someone who has been farming a long time, not someone just starting out, and certainly not to someone wanting to sell to less established markets"—not farmers supplying regional or local markets, in other words. "Farmers and retirees survive on a razor's edge." With that he lifted the knife, sharp side up. "Agriculture is risky enough, and landlords increasingly need that rental income to survive, as most aren't farming anymore."

Tom's comments square with a 2014 survey of farmland owners in Iowa. Roughly 75 percent of all agricultural landlords in the state at the time were sixty-five years of age or older, and 18 percent were eighty-five or above.[10]

The USDA, to its credit, is at least trying. Since 2009, it has provided more than $100 million in funding for its Beginning Farmer and Rancher Development Program. (And yet, that $100 million over the course of eight years is a drop in the bucket compared with, for example, the $94.3 *billion* in taxpayer support for the corn industry from 1995 to 2014.[11] I did not say that members of Congress, the folks ultimately behind the appropriation of these monies, were trying very hard to solve the problem.) The USDA's Farm Service Agency also provides loans to cover operating expenses, to purchase farmland, or to buy livestock and equipment. I also know about dozens of small-farm training workshops and incubator farm programs. Helpful? Yes. Sufficient? Not even close.

What we really need are new land transfer strategies.

Becky and Lois are the owner-operators of a sixty-five-acre organic fruit, vegetable, beef, chicken, and egg farm in Vermont that has supplied surrounding schools, retirement centers, hospitals, restaurants, food cooperatives, and farmers' markets. In their late fifties, they are beginning to think seriously about "life after farming"—a phrase both of them used more than once during our time together. Another favorite phrase of theirs was "wanting to have our cake and eat it too." By the end of our interview, I had suggested that they adopt one more: "Sometimes dreams do come true."

Our interview began with us seated in the kitchen of the rustic A-frame house that they had built together some twenty years earlier. I had just scooted my chair against a heavy wooden table, whose undercarriage I remember thinking could have substituted for a tornado shelter. Without even asking, Lois filled a kettle with water, set it on the stove, and struck a match. "I know you want coffee; me too," she said as she adjusted the flame. With the hum of gas and the *tick-tick* of heating metal in the background, she took a seat across the table and proceeded to ask herself the first question. "Should I start at the beginning, about why we got into farming?" Taking my smile and nod as affirmation, she began.

Like many, she talked about getting into agriculture to make a difference. Like many, she described the joy of working with her hands and growing food for the household and surrounding community. And, like many, Lois and her partner wanted to see what they had created be continued by the next generation. How they plan to go about it, however, was unlike anything I had heard, involving a novel agricultural conservation easement.

In a conventional agriculture conservation easement, a landowner places a deed restriction on his or her farm that requires it to remain in agriculture forever. This is quite common and relatively easy to put into place. Lois and Becky added a little twist to theirs. Three twists, actually, but who's counting?

In addition to stipulating that the land be farmed until the end of time, their easement requires (1) that the land is farmed in accordance with USDA organic certification standards, (2) that the owner is also the operator and that she or he must live on the farm, and (3) that more than half of the owner's income is derived from farming—hobby farmers need not apply.

They also established a resale restriction to ensure the land remains more affordable to beginning farmers than it otherwise would be if left to the dictates of land markets. Under the easement, when they decide to sell the land, it must be sold at the appraised agricultural value, rather than the always higher market value.

The trickiest element of the whole arrangement involves paying for the easement, the cost of which is determined by the difference between the agricultural and market values.

Becky and Lois will ultimately pocket this expense, which is why they call their plan an attempt to have their cake and eat it too. They could simply choose to forgo that revenue, place their land in the easement, and later sell it at the appraised agricultural value. But Becky and Lois are not wealthy. Moreover, when they bought the land, they paid something resembling market value for it, and they recounted bidding against a developer for it. The phrase "we paid a premium" came out of their mouths more than once.

Truth is, like most farmers they are strapped with considerable debt— they built a new barn a few years back that didn't help matters. This is why I am telling their story. I could see a lot of landowners getting behind an idea like this, even those who look at their land the way I look at my 401(k).

To cover the difference in price between the land's agricultural and housing market values, Becky and Lois are raising money with the help of crowdfunding platforms and fundraisers sponsored by area food cooperatives and restaurants. It is a community effort. Why? Because surrounding eaters want many of the same things that Lois and Becky want: local, organically grown food; short-distance commodity chains; a countryside inhabited by farmers who own their land; and a system of land tenure that helps ensure that those values carry forward to future generations.

Those who support this project know that merely buying the right foods cannot make these visions a reality. As one contributor to the crowdfunding platform told me, "We need to think systemically; this is a change, a big one, to business as usual."

I have mentioned this case to others who want to rethink the conventional sole ownership box. I will admit, it isn't exactly radical; after all, the future farmers lucky enough to work Becky and Lois's land will own it, and in a pretty conventional way. But innovation can take many forms, and even small changes can make big differences. This innovative land trust is an example of small-scale agriculture, sustainability, and foodscapes that engender connections between farmer and eater.

After I told a beginning farmers' organization about Becky and Lois's plan, members immediately started to think about how they could innovate further. "What if we sold shares?," someone asked, in order to make community members—the shareholders—partial owners. Another talked about how shareholders could fit into a nonprofit cooperative model, giving the farm tax-exempt status while still allowing the farmers to earn a salary. Another added, his voice firm, though I could sense his thoughts fluttering like trapped birds, "Maybe we could make the farm a learning center, or something that includes an agritourism element, or something done in conjunction with schools, or even rehabilitation centers."

Here's to examples of sharing that afford access, especially when they ruffle feathers.

It is one of the worst-kept secrets of the conventional foodscape: waste. Given our collective glorification of efficiency, it is frankly startling just how wasteful we are when it comes to what and how we eat. A recent report by attorneys in the Harvard Food Law and Policy Clinic estimates that approximately 40 percent of all food produced in the United States is wasted, which translates into 160 billion pounds of food annually. That is more than two million calories for every four-person household.[12]

There are a lot of reasons why we waste food: subsidies, which can lead to "overproduction" (an ironic term, given all the hungry people out there); social norms, which in some cultures encourage taking more than can be eaten; aesthetic standards, which require fruits and vegetables to look a certain way; infrastructure deficiencies, which are particularly problematic in lower income countries, where storage facilities are more likely to stand in disrepair.[13] But there is another reason, a big one: laws. Laws at the federal, state, and local levels make it difficult, impossible even, to get food that would otherwise go unused to those who need it.

Ask any retail or restaurant manager about the biggest risk associated with donating food waste, and chances are their angst can be summed up with one word: liability. The perception is that if you donate food to someone and they get sick or, worse, they die, you are potentially liable for their injury. Having that responsibility hanging over your head makes throwing away food the less risky option. Jacob Gersen, Harvard Law School professor and director of the Food Law Lab, put it this way: "Often it is easier to do the wrong thing; or rather, the law has made wasting food the only thing for many restaurants."[14]

Recognizing this, states and the federal government have passed what are known as Good Samaritan laws. These are designed to reduce liability, as long as donors are not grossly negligent or looking to make people sick. To further incentivize food donation, there are also tax benefits that come with sharing, but only if the donation is made to a charitable third party.

Activists and attorneys are trying to remove this middleman requirement. In a lot of cities, it is illegal to share food with the homeless, at least in public spaces. Stories abound of people getting fined for this. Take the one involving Arnold Abbott, a ninety-year-old World War II veteran who got busted by cops in Fort Lauderdale, Florida, *twice* in one week for doling out food to the homeless. Abbott was quoted in his local newspaper: "A policeman pulled my arm and said, 'Drop that plate right now,' like it was a gun."[15]

I want to focus on a less recognized barrier to corporate food sharing: the friction that exists between those with food, those who need it, and the intermediaries. A platform has emerged to smooth the rough spots between grocery stores and charities that want it: FoodCloud.

FoodCloud is a not-for-profit social enterprise—a legally recognized entity, on both sides of the pond, whose mission is to generate social dividends. This is not to say FoodCloud works for free. Retailers are charged a fee for this service, enough to pay FoodCloud employees a livable wage. In 2016, the company grew from working with 200 stores to more than 1,200 across the United Kingdom and Ireland. The receiving end, meanwhile, includes more than 3,300 community groups and charities.[16]

"FoodCloud differs from the food bank model in a number of ways. Perhaps the most obvious is in where we get our food from." This quote came from Maggie, a food safety inspector for the nonprofit. An acquaintance employed by Tesco Ireland gave me her phone number. Luck would have it that she was in London visiting her mum during a period when I also happened to be in the city. We met at a noisy Starbucks in the stately Kensington district. What stuck with me most about the interview was Maggie's voice. Low and soft, it seemed to operate at its own frequency, effortlessly cutting through all the background noise. It reminded me of a goose down feather, indescribably soft around the edges but with a stout, penetrating core. My digital recorder had no trouble catching every word.

Maggie again: "The food bank model involves getting food from manufacturers—the broken biscuits supply chain." This is a reference to donations that are unsuitable for retail, like a pummeled package of biscuits, which, to be clear, does not mean they are unsafe. (A few phone calls to food banks in Ireland told a slightly different story. As with food banks in North America, most of those I spoke with sourced from manufacturers, retailers, and distributors.) She went on to explain how FoodCloud receives its donations from retailers, "which means we tend to get greater quantity and often greater quality too; not something broken or banged up but something that might be approaching its 'best before' date but is otherwise perfect."

The platform works something like this. Businesses upload information about food destined for the landfill. Local charities are then notified. The first to accept the food is awarded the contract. To be eligible, charities must be registered; have, or have in the works, a food safety management system; and have staff with relevant food safety training.

FoodCloud's cofounders, Aoibheann O'Brien and Iseult Ward, appear keenly aware of the frictions that hamper sharing, tensions that are only amplified when talking about food.

Charities, by their very nature, are often ill equipped to handle food. Not all have the good fortune of being backed by entrepreneurial icons such as Bill and Melinda Gates. Instead, many operate on shoestring budgets, trying their best to reduce risk and liability while keeping up with safety regulations and practices. Without outside assistance, such expertise is often too much to ask from financially strapped charities. More than a pass-through middleman, FoodCloud is a genuine partner, helping to ease the burdens of all involved.

My conversation with Maggie continued down this track, about the need to make sure that, in her words, "sharing doesn't kill anyone." With that, she reached into her bag and pulled out a thin book published by the Food Standards Agency, a nonministerial department of the UK government responsible for protecting public health. Pointing at its cover, she added, "You can change what's in that book. You can also think about how to operate within existing law." She set the book down and pointed at her chest, which I took to mean *and that's where I come into the picture.*

"I think FoodCloud is an example of real outside-the-box thinking. We're changing business as usual but in a way that big business can get behind. What's more radical than that?" I am not sure if it is exactly radical, but it is certainly pragmatic. Given that it seems to be producing results, it's certainly worth exploring further.

The three of us were still on our first beer when Jeff observed, "I'm a chef because of what I *do*, not because of what I *own*." Jeff and I had recently been introduced by a friend, Peter, another food entrepreneur, who owned two food trucks—three guys enjoying beers and live music at a microbrewery in Fort Collins, Colorado. Peter's answer to what he called "the kitchen problem" was buying two 1999 Freightliner MT35s. (If you have ever seen a bread truck, that's what Peter bought.) His business, and his struggles to see things through, had been the subject of many previous conversations. Today, I was interested in learning more from Jeff about his business, a small jam company that shipped to stores in Colorado, Nebraska, Kansas, Wyoming, and New Mexico. Jeff sat to my left, Peter to my right.

With an unplugged version of Cheap Trick's "I Want You to Want Me" playing in the background, sans vocals, Jeff explained some initial challenges faced by his business. "When you dream about starting a business, you think *selling* your product is going to be the biggest challenge. I did. That was naïve; I never dreamed that *making* my product was going to be the hardest part. Hell, that was the *easiest* back when I was making jam for friends and family."

Comments like Jeff's are not uncommon, especially among food entrepreneurs rich with desire but less well off with what really matters in the ownership economy—cash, assets, credit, and equity. Commercial kitchens approved by the USDA and the federal Food and Drug Administration (FDA) are expensive to own. (The FDA regulates all foods and food ingredients introduced into or offered for sale in interstate commerce, with the exception of meat, poultry, and certain processed egg products, which are regulated by the USDA.) Thus, the very thing needed for making prepared food is out of reach for most aspiring chefs. At least, it is in the sole ownership economy. So you innovate, as by putting a kitchen in a truck: Peter's solution. Or, here's a thought: you can *share*.

Jeff sold roughly fifteen thousand jars of jam in 2016. That sounds like a lot. I remember my mom making jam every fall, and I recall how much work went into getting a couple dozen Ball canning jars of the stuff. Not that Jeff spent a lot of time in the kitchen. "I'm cooking for only a handful of hours a month," he told me, which made the expense of owning his own kitchen even more onerous—as with our cars: for many households, the car is the second biggest expense, yet it is not always regularly used. The rest of Jeff's time was spent dealing with marketing, packaging orders, answering phones, or doing any of the other hundred things small-business owners do to stay afloat. "Unlike food companies," he reminded me, "I have to do it all—cooking, accounting, branding, secretarial work, toilet cleaning."

Jeff had been connected with his current kitchen, and its owners, through an online marketplace for sharing kitchen space: the Food Corridor or, as National Public Radio called it, the "Airbnb of kitchens." The premise is brilliant on a number of levels, which gives me hope for its future.[17] Most kitchens sit idle for at least some part of the day, others for days or even weeks at a time. Think school kitchens over the summer or church galleys—that's a lot of square footage and stainless steel collecting dust. Why not put that idle capacity to work for entrepreneurs in need of kitchen space? As the platform's website reads, "The Food Corridor matches commercial kitchens who want to post their kitchen space with food businesses looking for a cooking place."[18]

It is not the Food Corridor per se that interests me here but what it enables, which brings me back to the seemingly offhanded, almost off-topic, comment that kicked off this section—the one in which Jeff identifies with being a chef because of what he *does* rather than because of what he *owns*.

The comment was not random, and it was too early in the evening for it to have been the beer talking. (As a researcher, I have a two-beer limit: never quote anybody after his or her second drink.) Jeff was trying to explain why he did not care if he ever owned his own kitchen. Beyond financial reasons, Jeff's self-worth and personal and professional identities were not threatened by the prospect of never owning his own commercial cooking equipment. There is actually something deeply profound about this admission.

Western legal theory assumes a "hierarchy of entitlements," in the words of Margaret Jane Radin, Henry King Ransom Professor of Law Emerita at the University of Michigan Law School.[19] According to this line of thought, people require ownership of possessions to achieve self-development.[20] Yet not all possessions have this effect. The hierarchy stretches out, from interchangeable assets, which do not warrant specific protections (like those pens in my desk), to personhood property, where the home sits at the pinnacle. As Radin explains, articulating the beliefs underling property law in the Anglo tradition, home is the "scene of one's history and future, one's life and growth," followed by the car, as automobiles "form the backdrop for carrying on private thoughts or intimate relationships, just as homes do."[21]

Look at how criminal law is structured. Punishments for invasion of a home almost always exceed the penalties imposed for invasions of other types of property.[22] Or take the Fourth Amendment and search and seizure law: generally the bar is higher for the state to enter or seize one's home than it is for commercial property. Bankruptcy law, too, regularly grants the home preferential protection.

The fact that Western legal thought even has an ownership hierarchy speaks volumes. Ownership represents the highest protection of the law because of its links to freedom, personhood, self-development, and autonomy.[23] To quote Shelly Kreiczer-Levy, a sharing economy jurist, "Property is a private space that is construed as free from interference of both the state and private actors. This spatial argument emphasizes control and exclusion as a way to draw boundaries between what is mine [where I am free] and what is outside my control."[24] Following conventional legal reasoning, then, the more you own, the more claim you have to being a self-developed, autonomous, and free person.

Does that sound right to you? Jeff didn't think so, either.

Later in the conversation, I steered things back to Jeff's comment about how his identity as a chef is less an aggregate of what he owns than a bundle of what he does. When I asked what he meant by that remark, he looked at his beer mug and rubbed its sweaty exterior with his thumb for a good four or five seconds.

"I can't say I've always felt this way," he explained, looking at me. "When you're brought up thinking things can be accomplished only one way, you can't blame anyone for measuring their self-worth by what they own." He went on to tell me about how as a child he had dreamed of owning his own restaurant. His first food venture was a lemonade and chocolate chip cookie stand at the age of seven.

His trust in the ownership economy to deliver well-being, material and otherwise, started to weaken a few years back, after he read *What's Mine Is Yours: The Rise of Collaborative Consumption* by Rachel Botsman and Roo Rogers.[25] Shortly after that, he started experimenting as a consumer with Uber, Airbnb, and the meal sharing platforms Josephine and Feastly. "Those experiences," he said—referring to peer-to-peer exchanges—"changed me." Staring at his second empty beer mug, which meant the recorder was about to be switched off, he hissed softy through his teeth, as if contemplating just how much to say.

"You don't buy a power drill for the sake of owning that specific piece of equipment. You buy it to make holes. *That's* what you want, the ability to make holes. That ability can be accomplished with or without ownership. And that ability is what makes us who we are, what gives us our identity and notions of self-worth."

As the bartender set down our fresh pours, Jeff closed the interview with this bit of wisdom: "I wonder if the world would be less of a shit-show if we shared more and owned a little less."

There is something hopeful about models of sharing that attempt to afford individuals access to goods. This is especially the case when that access can be had without the onerous costs of individual ownership, like the soul crushing burden of never ending debt—where it feels as if your kitchen owns you instead of the other way around. I can also get behind the idea of deriving self-worth and individual and collective identities not from what we own but instead by what we do.

I want to return to Jeff's final comment, about how we need to share more and own a little less. His thoughts cannot be abstracted from his connection to the Food Corridor. The Food Corridor is not solely concerned with access to material stuff, namely, kitchen space and equipment. This is part of the reason why I do not see it as the Airbnb of commercial kitchens, as the media often depict it.[26]

In the interest of full disclosure, I have known for a number of years the company's founder, Ashley Colpaart. In light of her upbringing, it is as if the Food Corridor was meant to be. "Raised on salsa and chips," she once told me. Her father worked in Silicon Valley in the 1990s as a hardware engineer—get it, *chips*—and her mom was a food entrepreneur, selling salsa at one point. Ashley thus knows all too well the challenges food entrepreneurs face and the power that comes from working together. Even when she talks about her dad making high-speed computer chips in their garage, the story is always one of a team effort.

The Food Corridor's leaders are therefore intent on creating platforms for the express purpose of sharing knowledge, as evidenced by NICK, the Network for Incubator and Commissary Kitchens. NICK is a closed group Facebook network, though the hurdles to entry are minimal—you need only ask to join and explain your interest. (In my case, I was approved two minutes later.) The social media platform of roughly 850 members, as of October 2017, is meant to be a space to share ideas around the intersections of food, kitchen space, and the circular economy. Members raise questions like "How do you charge for slow cooker use?," recognizing that a full rate would not be cost effective for a chef looking to braise lamb for eight hours. Or this one: "How does a recently enacted law mandating certain food prep practices within the city limits of Austin, Texas, help or hurt the local economy and those looking to share kitchen space?" Rethinking business as usual means *rethinking businesses' usual*. Doing that in the (virtual) presence of, and with the assistance of, others makes a lot more sense than trying to do it alone. You might even consider this network a community, in a loose social media sort of way. A weak network to be sure, but weak networks have their purpose too, especially when the aim is innovation, inclusivity, and avoidance of groupthink.[27]

Jeff realized this too, circling back to where our story began. There was a slight but detectable emphasis placed on the "we" in his final sentence: "I wonder if the world would be less of a shit-show if *we* shared more and owned a little less."

I think you're right, Jeff, especially if we learned to share more than just stuff.

CHAPTER 4
Social Trade-offs

I had been driving country roads for close to an hour. The dull purr of pavement eventually gave way to the steady rumble of gravel, like a hailstorm hitting the vehicle's underside. I saw the white tops of the iconic blue Harvestore silos peeking up over the dancing corn tassels well before the other buildings and farmhouse came into view. As I pulled into the half-mile-long driveway, a gentleman emerged from the airport hangar–like doors of the machine shed and walked toward his equipment laid out on the front lawn. It felt like the morning of a farm auction, before the crowd and auctioneer appear. There before me were ten John Deere implements, all laid out in two perfectly spaced rows.

As I walked from my rental car, the man stretched out his arms, standing among his equipment: "Welcome to tractor alley!" And so began my interview with Bart, a forty-something corn, soybean, and sorghum farmer whose operation is located in north central Kansas. I had found him through a friend of a friend. An acquaintance who manages a John Deere dealership in southern Iowa connected me with the manager of a John Deere dealership in south central Nebraska, who told me about Bart. Bart's "alley" was a flat and impeccably manicured four-acre lawn that stood between his house and the gravel road. The equipment was parked just far enough away that dust from passing cars couldn't reach his prized possessions. Green as far as the eye could see: John Deere, grass, surrounding cornfields, and, lest we forget, the money those diesel giants embodied. "More than two million," Bart said when asked how much these lawn ornaments cost.

Conceived by a Kansas City company that has been leasing combines for more than fifteen years, MachineryLink Sharing advertises itself as a sharing platform—it's called MachineryLink *Sharing*, after all. The firm promises to help farmers make money by renting, on a short-term basis, their equipment to those who cannot afford, or who choose not, to buy these machines outright. The arrangement therefore is not equivalent to Uber, even though the two companies are often portrayed by the media as analogous.[1] Bart does not drive fellow farmers around. His equipment is shipped, via big rig, to whoever is willing to pay the price.

Speaking of cost, it is not exactly cheap to rent equipment through this sharing platform. "Generally," Bart told me, "you'll spend anywhere between $20,000 and $50,000 to use my equipment." Later that day, he showed me an invoice that backed up this claim. It was for a tractor he had leased for 200 hours at a cost of $38,000 to some guy in Washington State. That might sound like a lot—it *is*. But for most of Bart's customers it is still a deal, a point he emphasized more than once.

Taking back the invoice, Bart slipped into the staccato speech pattern of a rehearsed sales pitch. "MachineryLink covers repairs almost 100 percent of the time; oil changes are fully covered; belt costs are split fifty-fifty. If the equipment is down for more than forty-eight hours, they'll get you another one in just a day or two. With MachineryLink, you're also getting peace of mind."

The practice isn't exactly new. Farmers have been leasing equipment for generations, borrowing it from one another for even longer. The platform's innovation lies in allowing farmer-to-farmer leasing, versus business-to-farmer.

MachineryLink offers access to equipment in a sector plagued by financial barriers that can be as insurmountable as Mount Everest in the winter. As if the rising price of farmland weren't bad enough, just *one* of Bart's tractors cost more than what people in the nearest town were paying for houses. I know car dealers whose inventory does not match the cost of what Bart has on his front lawn. And then there are his routine maintenance costs. A single tire could cost as much as $5,000, times *eight* for those eight-wheel-drive behemoths.

MachineryLink offers significant advantages, reducing the costs of doing business for some producers. Farming is a business with incredibly tight margins, and they are only getting tighter. Average U.S. farm incomes have been on a steady decline for generations, dropping by 36 percent in 2015 alone.[2] MachineryLink is a platform with the potential to turn a red end-of-year ledger black for a group repeatedly getting the shaft. These upsides, however, should not keep us from asking about the downsides—particularly any effects beyond the financial ones.

My time with Bart concluded with a tour of his new four-track John Deere tractor—it has four tracks, each in the shape of a triangle, instead of wheels. From the cab, I saw another vehicle's dust rising in the distance before I heard it. The truck came into view seconds before it passed. "That's Scott," Bart told me as the sound of the big block diesel engine receded, overtaken by the wind, rustling leaves, and the occasional *moo*—Bart also milks. "He's not a huge fan of this piece of equipment." *What's not to like?* I thought while fiddling with the computer positioned to the right of the tractor's chair, as in cop cars.

Getting up, I asked what he meant. Bart took off his hat and crumpled it in his hand. Then he began using it to swat at the empty air, chasing imaginary flies. After a couple swipes, he opened it back up and placed it atop his head, slightly off-center. He proceeded to tell a story. It was about him, I soon learned, even though he referred to himself in the third person.

I was told about two neighbors who used to borrow each other's equipment. The practice had begun with their fathers and continued until recently, when one neighbor started using a sharing platform and traded up his older implements for newer models. The neighbors, of course, were Bart and Scott.

Now that Bart was trucking his new pieces of equipment across the country, they were no longer available to be borrowed, or what some would call *shared*. This, in his words, "hasn't exactly been a plus as far as neighborly relations are concerned."

This was neither the first nor the last time I heard stories in which formal sharing actually pushed people apart rather than bringing them together. As Bart described the rift with Scott, his explanation was telling. He seemed to be saying the platform encouraged the *commodification* of relationships: "I can make $20,000 or $30,000, or I can let my neighbor use it for free. You do the math. Unless I start charging the guy"—he was talking about Scott here—"a comparable rate, the tractor's going to the guy who's going to pay."

Here, then, are more reasons to temper our sharing triumphalism with a critical eye, realizing that such exchanges are not without trade-offs. As with this one: sharing more *this way* means sharing less *that way*.

You might think that we know a lot about the sharing economy's role in fostering community. It is called the *sharing* economy, after all. But we have been putting emphasis on the other word, which explains why we know far more about the economic potential of these emerging practices than we do about what they mean for civil society.

Given their relative newness, we're only beginning to understand their noneconomic impacts: one of the earliest studies to examine the societal consequences of these newfangled platforms dates back only a few years, to 2012. The research examined the experience of members of Zipcar, a for-profit car sharing enterprise.[3] With Zipcar, members rent cars for as little as, to take those available on the campus of my university (Colorado State), $7.50 per hour. Members can use an app to locate their automobile—they're often scattered throughout designated neighborhoods—by honking its horn. Through the app, users can also unlock the car's doors and start the vehicle. The study found that the platform did nothing to build users' attachment to the community, which should not be surprising, considering that a person can rent and return a Zipcar without ever coming into contact with another human. Convenient? Yes. Community building? Not a chance.

But then again, we ought to expect that from platforms intentionally designed to *reduce* social interaction.

Most sharing platforms involve at least some social contact. With Uber, a proprietary platform facilitates the exchange—so efficiently, in fact, that communication is not necessary to complete the transaction. The platform "tells" the driver where to go, and the company automatically charges the trip to the rider's credit card. Drivers are at least encouraged to be convivial, and riders, if for no other reason than to be courteous, generally reciprocate. There's no obvious reason to think these platforms harm social relations. But if the earlier story about Scott and Bart is at all generalizable, then we have an obligation to learn more.

In his late twenties, Nathan reminded me of a character in a Tim Burton movie. His style was a cross between Goth and vintage 1930s gangster—pale skin, jet-black hair in need of an oil change, dark double-breasted jacket, and black fedora. Nate was a college student, and he and his closest friends could be considered heavy users of food sharing platforms, claiming to get between four and six of their meals weekly through them. Nate's platform of choice was Feastly, though he also mentioned occasionally using Josephine and Eatwith.

"He doesn't expect me to pay, of course. But still, my eating at his house might be keeping a paying customer out." Nathan was telling me about his longtime friend Jack. Jack had started selling food regularly through Feastly, one of the better known and longer established food sharing platforms. Meals generally cost from $25 to $75. Of that, Feastly takes a 20 percent cut, for the platform and the vetting of cooks to make sure the food is up to par. The chefs keep the rest.

It is a pretty straightforward business model. You go online and purchase a spot at someone's table for a specific meal. And then, at a prearranged time, you go to the chef's house and eat—a dinner party you pay to attend where you don't know anyone.

Nathan expressed sentiments that I had heard from others. Jack used to host "truly legendary"—Nathan's words—dinner parties: five or six courses, mixed drinks, games, and comradery. "Then his weekend nights started to be booked with *paying* dinner parties." Nathan slapped his hands down on the wooden tabletop between us with the word "paying."

Jack still has friends over for dinner, Nathan among them. Yet this rarely happens during weekends anymore, as those tend to be his most profitable nights. Nathan explained: "The gang rarely all gets together anymore for these meals, with people having to work the next morning." He admits this is more of an inconvenience than something worth losing sleep over. Yet Feastly has caused the group real angst.

Nathan spent a good deal of time trying to explain how the feeling of these dinner parties changed—he used the terms "feel" and "feeling" repeatedly. "First, you can't help but feel like you ought to be paying, given that someone else could be eating there, and paying for it, if it weren't for your presence." Nathan and his friends soothed their consciences by bringing more to the dinners than they had before. "Whereas before I'd bring a bottle of wine, I usually bring a couple bottles now, or a bottle and some appetizers."

This guilt does not seem entirely unfounded, given one of Jack's new favorite topics of conversation at these dinners, when he finds time to host them. According to Nathan, "Jack likes to announce how much he would have made had he charged us for the meal."

I decided to get Jack's side of the story, a delicate prospect, since I had no intention of throwing Nathan under the bus by revealing his concerns about their friendship.

Pulling into Jack's driveway, I immediately spotted the signature tail fins, and then the rest of it. A fully restored '57 Chevy Bel Air was parked in the garage. Remembering Nathan's style, I was expecting to meet another twenty-something rocking the retro look. Instead, a young man sporting a high-and-tight military-style haircut stood at the door, wearing khakis and a polo shirt. After welcoming me, he guided me to his kitchen, an open space with a large table at one end and an island in the middle, followed by a peninsula that connected to the rest of the counter and cabinet space.

I had told Jack over the phone that I wanted to talk with him about his experiences using Feastly, as I had learned from a friend that he was having considerable success with the platform. Given that Jack had only an hour before he needed to leave, we made quick pleasantries and got right to work.

He was making between $500 and $700 per month, after Feastly's commission and the cost of the food. He told me he had always wanted to be a chef. The platform allowed him to live out a childhood fantasy, though he doubted he would continue it over the long term. He was planning instead to go to law school and become a real estate attorney.

Ultimately, it was he who directed the conversation to the subject of his friends and their increasingly infrequent dinner parties. He had been hosting parties with the same group since graduating from high school eight years before. At the high point, he was having friends—mostly the same friends—over twice a month. That had changed about a year ago, when he started using Feastly regularly.

"I wouldn't say I'm choosing money over friends—*really*." His downcast eyes and the fact that "really" came out a whole two octaves higher made me wonder if he was trying to convince himself as much as me. He admitted, "If I have become money focused, it is because I have to; that stove isn't going to pay for itself." Later, he added, "I can have my friends over, or I can have paying customers over who will help me recoup expenses."

Jack had bought a high-end commercial stove about six months earlier, thinking his new gig would help subsidize its cost. I was not surprised to hear this. All this talk about how peer-to-peer platforms reduce consumption—why buy a drill when you can use someone else's?—misses the fact that sharing can also *increase* consumption by creating new revenue streams. I had heard about this more than once in the context of Uber—of someone buying a second car, perhaps even one a step up from what they could otherwise afford, hoping their income from this platform would cover the difference. I also saw this with Bart and MachineryLink. Before joining the platform, Bart had owned one tractor that was less than twenty-four months old. When I spoke with him, he had *six* pieces of equipment that were more or less new.

By the halfway mark of the interview, I felt pretty confident that Nathan had been telling the truth when he said Jack liked to announce during dinner parties how much he would have made had he charged for the meal. Jack had already admitted to being fairly calculating about whom to have over—paying strangers or nonpaying friends. After all, that stove wasn't going to pay for itself. Later, he confessed to "wishing [his friends] would cough up a few bucks when they came over to eat" so he could spend more time with them. I then *knew* Nathan's descriptions were spot-on.

"Never mix friendship and business." Peer-to-peer platforms give new meaning to the saying, reminding us that in commodifying previously *private* actions—sharing tractors, meals, rides—we risk crowding out those actions, and the people attached to them, for opportunities that pay. I am not suggesting Jack's transformation is representative of your typical peer-to-peer chef. But it is a reminder of what can happen when you start putting a price tag on activities that previously didn't come with one.

So what is gained and what is lost through platforms such as Feastly and Josephine? Again, our understanding of them is largely limited to their *economic* impacts.[4] We can cite, for example, how "in 2015, the sharing economy created 60,000 jobs in the United States and attracted a total of $15 billion in financing," while projecting that the sector is expected to "generate $335 billion in revenue for 2025."[5]

We have to be able to say more.

These "side hustles"—there's a term to drop if you want to sound like a player in the sharing economy—can reduce barriers for aspiring entrepreneurs. The restaurant industry is not for the faint of heart or stomach. In conventional foodscapes, this means owning expensive space and kitchen equipment and then figuring out a way to pay for it all while hoping against hope to eke out a profit. Roughly 60 percent of these businesses fail in their first year, and only 20 percent survive to see their fifth anniversary.[6] Can sharing substitute for business acumen, knowledge about food safety, or the ability to cook? Of course not. Sharing is not a panacea. But it does make entry into the food business less daunting.

What's less clear is these platforms' potential to build community, in the immediate term, at least. Remember, we are talking about one-off exchanges here. But perhaps the societal value of these exchanges should not be measured exclusively by their ability to generate durable relationships. Hoping that sharing platforms create friends could, in fact, be seen as putting the cart before the horse, especially given the state of the world today. It is hard to make friends with people you cannot stand being in the same room with, or who you think are "drug dealers, criminals, rapists," if we are talking about forging friendships with Mexicans and your feelings align with those of President Trump.[7]

Can we say anything about whether these platforms make people more comfortable being around others, especially others different from themselves?

I first met Ben while eating dinner at a stranger's house. We were part of the same meal sharing dinner party, friends of a mutual friend. Seated next to each other for the entire meal, we had plenty of time to get to know one another. By the end of the night, we had exchanged contact information and agreed to meet the next day to discuss Ben's experiences with Cookapp, the platform responsible for our introduction.

We met the next morning at eight o'clock in a cute six-table café, complete with the little bell on the door, decorative pressed metal on the ceiling, and what looked like original art deco floor tile. First, we reviewed what had happened the night before. We both agreed that the food, and the goat curry in particular, was spectacular. We also talked about cricket—the game, not the insect. Our host hailed from New Zealand and had cricket memorabilia scattered throughout the house—vintage wickets and stumps and a signed photograph of New Zealand cricketer Brendon "Baz" McCullum.

Then our coffee came, and we got to the business at hand.

"I wouldn't say I've made many friends from it—excluding yourself, maybe one or two others." Ben had been using Cookapp for more than a year. The platform first launched in Buenos Aires, Argentina, in May 2013, becoming available to New Yorkers in February 2014. It is a meal sharing platform, not all that different from the likes of Eatwith, Feastly, and Josephine.

In the case of Cookapp New York, eaters come to the "restaurant," which in this city is typically an apartment, for good food and sometimes awkward conversation, all for less than what they would spend eating out. Guests are encouraged to make a "suggested donation"—around fifty bucks, according to Ben, depending on whether liquor is included or the event is BYO, "bring your own." The "suggested donation" wording is a workaround to exempt these practices from New York City's health department policy, which does not allow selling meals out of a residence.

Ben admitted to using Cookapp and other platforms like it about once a week. When I asked him to describe his experiences, I was surprised by what he recalled. I was expecting him to talk about the food. Instead, he focused on the hosts and other guests. Their unexpected quirks, like a fascination with cricket. Their religion: a subject that was not raised with any frequency, though over one meal a host's Wiccan identity became a subject of conversation—"I'm still not 100 percent sure what Wicca is, but what I heard involved stuff I could get behind." Nationality: during the previous eight meals, Ben had met people from Iran, Italy, Brazil, and Saudi Arabia.

In hindsight, and after talking with others about their experiences with these platforms, I realized there was nothing extraordinary about this. Others too were more concerned with whom they met than what they ate, especially when those encountered were different in some way.

Ben was now reflecting on his earlier comment about not having made many friends through these experiences. "Sometimes it's not friends we need as much as opportunities, opportunities to get to know people different from ourselves." It was an interesting insight. We want our sharing opportunities to build social networks, to create *friends*. But it is hard to make friends with people if you fear or hate them.

With that, the conversation turned as we discussed how growing one's network of friends might actually contribute to today's societal ills. Ben again: "Racists have friends, who are mostly all racist too. Growing that circle of nastiness isn't going to help anyone." This brought us back to the issue of *whom* we are befriending.

Earlier, Ben had talked positively about meeting people different from himself, meetings made possible by meal sharing platforms. Those experiences were no doubt weighing on his mind at this very moment.

Elbows on the table, holding the stainless steel napkin dispenser in both hands, he gazed at his reflection. The image gazing back was warped and contorted—I know because I could see my own reflecting on the opposite side. He studied the distortion for several seconds before adding, without looking up, "I would like to see what would happen if someone like that sat down and broke bread with an undocumented immigrant. Or, better, a Muslim." Looking up, he added, with a small chuckle, "Perhaps that is precisely what they need."

It is important that we create opportunities for people to work together. Our future depends on it. But this requires a willingness to actually work together. You cannot force collaboration, any more than you can force two people from different backgrounds to eat together at the same table and have a conversation. Yet what if people came to that table for the prospect of good, affordable food? What if getting to know people different from you were an unintended side effect? Might people let their guard down long enough to see the person across from them as *a person* and not as, for example, someone associated with drug dealers, criminals, and rapists?

If you think we ought to build a wall between the United States and Mexico, or if you think one group is culturally superior to another, I have a pretty good idea of who you are going to choose to collaborate with, namely, others who think and pray as you do and perhaps even look like you. That is exactly the direction we *don't* want to go as we seek to build sharing communities.

I soon learned that Ben's comments about racists befriending racists were rooted in a very personal example. Leaning forward over the table, in a voice that was definitely a few decibels lower than usual, he told me about a racist uncle whom he referred to coldly as "the butt-hole."

His uncle, I learned, is a popular guy and has been for a long time. Prom king. High school football captain. But beyond *that* cliché, he is, according to Ben, "just a really well-liked guy, if you like that sort of thing." That last dig is a reference to his uncle's largely homogeneous network of connections. His friends, a crew of like minded compatriots, all get their news from the same television and radio programs. They even look the same. Ben pulled his smartphone from his pocket and showed me his uncle's Facebook page. One group picture looked like a scene on the set of a Spike TV program about custom motorbikes—Harleys, wraparound sunglasses, jeans, black shirts, and faces sporting facial hair and grimaces more than grins. And, of course, they were all white. "They all believe in the same politics," Ben added.

"I don't hate the guy," Ben explained as he returned his phone to his pocket, continuing, "I just wish he'd have these experiences." By "these experiences," he meant those not quite peer-to-peer encounters that Ben found so rewarding, meetings that were created through food sharing platforms. He added, "I can't see how he could still hold some of the views he holds if he got to know the people he's vilifying."

With that, he looked up and smiled. Then the smile turned into a full-fledged grin, spreading from one ear to the other until he looked like a clam just opened. "He would never intentionally break bread with someone not like him—not, how do I say it . . . white. *Can't have illegals in our country!*" Ben intoned, his voice dropping an octave and becoming gravelly as he impersonated his uncle. "But maybe," back to

Ben's voice again, "he would if it were under the pretext of getting some good, old-fashioned home cooked food."

As Gandhi explained, the enemy is fear. We think it is hate, but it's fear. Fear is born of ignorance. We should always be vigilant when it comes to scouting for practices with the potential to reduce ignorance about, and thus fear and hate toward, others.

Here's to appealing to the better angels of our nature, and to finding ways to keep them well fed.

CHAPTER 5

Putting Shared Technologies to Work

A little known irony about Thomas Jefferson and his agrarian ideal: successful farm ownership during his presidency was entirely dependent on seed *sharing*.

There were no Stokes Seeds catalogues for early U.S. immigrants. Settlers used what they brought with them from the Old Country or what they acquired through trade with others. But this was a new land, with a different climate and soils. Many of those early crops failed as the seed proved ill-suited for the realities of their new home.

Affluent landowners pooled their resources to overcome these hurdles, importing seed and adapting it to the New World's environment. These seed saving and sharing networks were called "societies." Seed did not become widely available to farmers, other than through their personal networks, until 1819. In that year, the secretary of the treasury called upon all U.S. ambassadors and military officers stationed overseas to collect seed from their posts and bring it back so it could be shared freely. This officially became the responsibility of the U.S. Patent Office in 1839, after the commissioner of patents, Henry Ellsworth, secured funding from Congress to collect and distribute agricultural seed and statistics.

How was this facilitated? The U.S. Postal Service. Ten years in, the program was distributing 60,000 packages of seed annually. By 1855, the millionth seed parcel had been sent.[1] The U.S. Department of Agriculture took up the practice with its formation in 1862. This was one of the agency's early charges: the procurement, propagation, and distribution of plant varieties for the nation's farmers. By the end of the century, the agency was shipping approximately 1 billion free packages of seed annually.[2]

There were seed companies during the 1800s, such as Stokes Seeds, which started in 1881. But most seed businesses were short lived. The fact that the seed reproduced itself meant companies had little incentive to invest in increasing a plant's vigor or yield, given that it could be replicated for free. Once an improvement was made, and the seed sold, everyone had access to it. Try getting rich off *that* business model.

The American Seed Trade Association was founded in 1883. After decades of lobbying, the group was able to convince Congress to end the free seed program in 1924. It is no coincidence that around that time the first hybrid seed entered the market: hybrid corn.

Hybrid corn outperformed traditional varieties by 100 percent, with yields in the early twenty-first century 400 times greater than those reported in the 1930s.[3] Its seed also came with an added benefit, from the industry's perspective, at least. Hybrid corn's progeny never achieved the same yields as did the parent plant. This made the innovation a boon to seed companies. Farmers could have saved the seed if they wanted to. But why? The money saved would have been more than offset by the money lost at market. Farmers using second-generation hybrid seed could expect yields lower than those of crops from traditional seed varieties. (They could have tried to produce their own hybrid seed, but the formulas have always been a trade secret.) This marks the start of the commercialization of the seed industry, now one of the most concentrated sectors of the entire conventional foodscape (the image in figure 5.1 comes from 1917).

FIGURE 5.1

We have come a long way since the days of free seed programs and seed societies. Post offices have disappeared from the seed sharing landscape. Yet, another community pillar is now opening up seed "ownership" to everyone. The library.

As libraries around the country expand their collections to include e-books, digitized audio media, and online video streaming materials, many are also making available to patrons some of the oldest technology of all: seed. Until recently, the checkout procedure at seed libraries looked something like this: you selected seed to take home, grew them, harvested the fruits, and made sure to return some seed from your harvest to the library. That was pretty standard procedure until a number of seed libraries across the nation were served with cease and desist letters. Turns out that process is illegal in certain states. Yes, in some states you can legally buy and grow marijuana, but if you hope to start up a seed sharing library, be prepared to have state agents knocking on your door.

The most unsettling case that I know of occurred in 2014, when the Pennsylvania Department of Agriculture informed a seed library that it was breaking a law—the state's Seed Act of 2004. The seed library, its officials were told, fell under the definition of a "seed distributor," which meant it needed to start acting like one. It was required to meet stringent labeling requirements. The labels needed to be in English and had to clearly state the plant's species name or commonly accepted name. For hybrid varieties, the label needed to state whether the seed had been treated. Finally, labels were required to include the name and address of the seed sharing entity. As a seed distributor, the library was also told it must conduct germination and purity analyses. The process was quite a bit different from the way the library was used to handling things, when seed was treated like books. Some seed samples were bought, others donated. Once seed was obtained, the library slapped a bar code on it and sat it on a shelf.

Seed acts are generally well intentioned. At one level, they protect consumers from unscrupulous seed vendors—thus the laws are both well intentioned and *needed* in exchanges motivated centrally by a desire for profit. Yet that does not describe the circumstances surrounding, or motivations underlying, seed libraries. Their seed is not for sale, and exchanges are not commercial. Instead, behaviors are governed by norms rooted in trust, reciprocity, and empathy. This is a far cry from the dog-eat-dog corporate world, where shareholder happiness and market share are priorities number one and two.

Back in Pennsylvania, tensions flared when the Cumberland County commissioner, Barbara Cross (her identity is a matter of public record), found a way to drop the t-bomb into the conversation. "Agri-terrorism is a very, very real scenario," she was quoted as saying in an interview, adding, "You've got agri-tourism on one side and agri-terrorism on the other."[4] As you could imagine, being identified as potential terrorists did not go over well among the activists trying to make seed saving and sharing legal in the state.

The seed library was eventually allowed to remain open, after it was agreed that gardeners would not be required to bring seed back to the library. Stipulating that patrons must return seed would have made the loan a transaction, technically speaking, not a giveaway.

Where, then, does the library get its seed, if not from the community? The seed provided must be commercially packaged. Not exactly a fairy-tale ending, I know. To their credit, officials of the Pennsylvania Department of Agriculture did tell library officials that they could host seed swap events and still remain in compliance with the 2004 Seed Act, thus creating opportunities for real seed sharing.

The Pennsylvania case is but one of many dealing with seed libraries. Others had more hopeful resolutions.

In September 2016, Assembly Bill 1810 was signed into law in California.[5] The bill, known among seed saving activists as the Seed

Exchange Democracy Act,[6] amends the "seed law" chapter of the state's Food and Agricultural Code to exempt seed libraries from burdensome testing and labeling requirements.

Marvin, a self-described "seed sharing activist, gardener, and attorney," helped craft A.B. 1810. Like others I spoke with in the seed library movement (my term, but those involved seemed to like it), Marvin was quick to point out that seed sharers are "as far from being agri-terrorists as one can be." He continued, crescendoing until the final word, which came out in a falsetto, "This has everything to do with increasing biodiversity and reducing food insecurity, and yet people have the gall to call us *terrorists?*"

With that, he grabbed the laptop on his desk and slid it toward himself. He typed for a few seconds before turning the screen to face me. "Critics of seed libraries need to be honest with who they're really looking to protect," he said, back in his normal baritone, while pointing at the screen. I was being shown a legal document. Across the top, in a fancy calligraphy font, were the words "In The Supreme Court of the United States." I was looking at a legal brief, filed by twenty-one different agriculture industry organizations, for the 2013 Supreme Court case *Bowman v. Monsanto Co.*

It was a U.S. Supreme Court decision in which the Court unanimously affirmed the decision that the patent exhaustion doctrine does not give farmers the right to plant and grow saved patented seed without the patent owner's consent. "Look here." Marvin was pointing at the screen. "It reads, and I quote, 'Early seed breeders had little incentive to make costly investments in developing more productive plants because the free seed program crowded private breeders from the marketplace.'" With that, he slammed the laptop shut. "That's what we're up against, the idea that seed sharing of any sort cuts into their precious market share. Seed companies don't care about improving food security. They're just looking after their bottom line."

With more than 300 seed lending libraries in existence in the United States, the subject of their legality is starting to be scrutinized by state authorities. "As with anything," Marvin told me, "the government generally doesn't bother with enforcement if there's only a few random cases here and there. Now that seed libraries are becoming a thing, a movement, agencies are beginning to take notice. They're not flying under the radar anymore."

Fortunately, activists have a lot of models to draw from as they challenge the idea that seed lending libraries are the legal equivalent to seed distributors. The recently passed California law follows similar laws passed in Minnesota, Nebraska, and Illinois, all in a matter of eighteen months. In North Carolina, seed libraries are legal thanks to a blanket seed sharing exemption that applies to all nonprofits. Alabama has on the books an exemption for anybody who sells up to $3,000 worth of seed, which means you are even allowed to sell a small quantity of seed if you want.

With the end of our interview in sight, I asked Marvin to sum up the main takeaway from his experiences: a background that ranged from helping to get A.B. 1810 passed to consulting with seed activists in other states. He had obviously given the topic some thought, because while he answered immediately, what he said had an equal mix of lament and bite to it. "To think seed libraries are essentially illegal in some parts of this country tells you something about what our priorities are. We're a nation built on seed sharing. But we've moved so far in the other direction."

Frustrated, Marvin clenched both hands into a fist until his knuckles turned white. He continued: "When we create laws, we don't think about how they impact sharing because sharing is now so far from our minds and from what we do. That's not right."

Brice, with his Vans shoes, fedora, purple hair, and bright green glasses, did not look like your typical seed saver. I met with him outside at a picnic table, under the shade of a large oak. The tree dripped with life, its branches days away from erupting with leaves that would mark another year, a new ring in its core a testament to a long life. Spring. In another month, the seed in Brice's hand would begin its metamorphosis. Within a single lunar phase, it would be breaking through the soil.

I started the interview by asking Brice about what drew him to seed saving. "This is about the most precious resource of all." He was not talking only about the seed packet clenched in his hand. He lifted both arms up, giving me flashbacks to watching *The Price Is Right* as a kid, when a contestant was being shown a prize for the first time. He was clearly talking about, well, *everything*—the seed, the property we were on, the people attached to this space, and the knowledge attached to those people. "It's about setting knowledge free. With that you can do anything, which is precisely why Big Food has done everything it can to lock it up."

When talk turns to the sharing economy, attention is often directed to the sharing of things—goods, food, equipment, even land and buildings. What tends to get missed is that peer-to-peer sharing works only when those peers *know what they're doing*.

I was sitting with Brice on the grounds of the Seed Savers Exchange. SSE is tucked up in the northeastern corner of Iowa, a mere fifteen-minute drive to the Minnesota border. (It is also a twenty-five-minute drive, in the other direction, to my hometown, where my parents still live.) SSE consists of an 890-acre farm, known as Heritage Farm. A nonprofit organization, SSE maintains a collection of more than 20,000 heirloom and open-pollinated vegetable, herb, and plant varieties, plus over 1,000 varieties of heritage apple trees. It is one of the largest nongovernmental seed banks in the United States. It is a *living* seed bank: every year, SSE grows out selected varieties—hence the name, *Heritage* Farm—to refresh its supply.

With its barn, gardens, gravel drive, and wildlife, this is not your typical seed bank—a far cry from the Fort Knox–like facility near my office at Colorado State University, where the U.S. federal seed vault is located. This government operated facility—the building is nondescript, beige, and dotted with security cameras—looks about as welcoming as a federal prison, which is basically what it is, for a very specific class of nonhuman inmates. SSE, meanwhile, expects and even welcomes visitations and freely releases members from its general population. But more than that, it promotes cohabitation and collaborative learning. Its aim is not just to lock away the "assets" but also to share them, bringing people, seed, and experiences together.

Brice and I stood in front of the visitors' center. With its red paint and white trim, the newish building looked like a barn. "I've been coming to the Exchange since the 1990s and have attended most of the events," he said. "We're a family, and I'm including these little guys in that group." Brice looked down at the seed in his open hand. One day they would produce Dragon's Tongue beans, beautiful yellow pods streaked with purple.

Brice went on to tell me about how members request seed from one another, either online through a members-only portal, or by more conventional means, like by picking up a phone and asking for them. This led to a discussion about SSE sponsored events, spurred on by a question about how members (and seed) get to know each other. So many events: Start with Seed; Apple Grafting School; Spring Plant Sale; Spring Garden School; The Garden Ecosystem; Weed Dating (get it, *Weed* Dating—ha!); Conference and Campout; Seed School; Community Appreciate Day; Cooking with Heirlooms; Benefit Concert; Seed Stories Workshop; Harvest Festival; Winter on the Farm.[7]

Later that day, I met Sarah. Claiming to be in her mid-sixties but looking a solid ten years younger, she had been coming to SSE events since the late 1990s. Sarah owned and operated a bed-and-breakfast in Milwaukee, raised chickens, and, not surprisingly, was an avid gardener.

When she reached out her hand to shake mine, I was struck by the juxtaposition of well manicured, painted nails and the dirt caked under some of them.

Sarah spent a good deal of our conversation emphasizing, in her words, "how knowledge does not take a backseat to seed here; the two are inseparable."

It is one thing to share an object. In some respects, sharing *things* is the easy part—though, as we saw with seed libraries, what should be simple can quickly become difficult, especially when vested interests are thrown into the mix. Seed requires know-how to be of any use. Sarah again: "You can't just look at a seed and know how deep it ought to be planted, or how much water it needs, or how much space between each is needed, or what soil type it works best in. Gardening is as much an art as it is a science. You have to do it before you really know what works in your garden."

You have to do it before you really know what works in your garden. If you are a gardener, you know what Sarah is talking about. Saving and sharing seed is like riding a bike, in that you have to do it to know it. Try telling someone how to ride a bike who has never ridden one before. It doesn't work. Similarly, understanding seed requires in-person help, someone who can (sometimes literally) hold your hand as you get a feel for the process.

Peer-to-peer sharing is one piece of this. But what we also need, especially when talking about food, is peer-to-peer *mentoring*. Sarah again: "The most successful food sharing platforms—and for me, I define 'successful' as those that improve food access and food sovereignty—the successful ones need to provide access to *skills* as much as goods." For emphasis, she pointed two of those earth-encrusted, painted fingernails at my chest.

Good point. Who cares if communities share seed, or whether or not seed libraries are legal, if no one knows how to garden or to prepare the produce once harvested? Sharing cannot be just about an exchange of idle stuff, though that is how it is typically framed by advocates—for example, "Got stuff lying around? Share it!" We need to recognize that wanting access to someone else's idle stuff is predicated on knowing what to do with it once you have it.

Sarah was also involved in the Open Source Seed Initiative. The initiative, commonly known as OSSI, was "inspired," to quote from the group's website, "by the free and open source software movement that has provided alternatives to proprietary software."[8] To be a part of the initiative, breeders promise that the seed they help produce will be available to other breeders and that the seed can be saved and planted in future seasons. As you will recall, patents and technology agreements outlaw these elements when it comes to most commercial seed.

Launched in 2014, OSSI has grown into a global network of university scientists, not-for-profit organizations, farmers, and freelance plant breeders. Within its first month of existence, over two hundred orders flowed in from eight countries.[9] In June 2015, after a three-day meeting near Hyderabad, India, Apna Beej (Hindi for "Our Seeds") was formed, an OSSI sister organization—also known as Open Source Seed System India (OSSSI).

This brings me back to Sarah's earlier point about how seed and knowledge are inseparable. One problem with the corporate control of seed is that we are not talking only about locking up seed, which is problematic enough. When you have more than one-third of a vegetable's genetic material privatized, as in the case of carrots, it becomes difficult for breeders to innovate. The companies holding those patents will claim that patents stimulate innovation. But the fact is, unless a trait is wildly profitable, there is no incentive for seed firms to use it. Necessity isn't really the mother of invention. Profit is. One of the most problematic aspects of placing all our eggs in the private sector (i.e., profit motivated) basket is that those most in need of food access and innovation—the poor—will never see its benefits. Why? It's a matter of simple economics. Catering to that population alone will never make shareholders rich.

Patents also lock away knowledge and discourage the community building that happens when that know-how is shared. As Sarah put it, "No one just saves seed. If you save seed, you also talk with others about the seed they have, the traits that work, about planting and fertilizer schedules." With that, she reached deep into the front pocket of her jeans—forearm deep, which made it look as if she were scratching her knee. After a few seconds of digging, she pulled out a handful of small yellowish seed. *Millet*, I thought. (It was, I later learned.) Her hand immediately went to mine, in a "Here, take it!" gesture. She added, "And you share it."

Here is to saving, sharing, learning, and growing communities as much as plants.

Multiple-choice question. A hacker club is (A) a group of slasher film aficionados; (B) a whacking device with a sharp edge; or (C) a network of like minded software and hardware enthusiasts. If the answer isn't obvious, it soon will be.

A quick internet search can verify their abundance, though, as I learned, not all hacker clubs announce their identity online—a fact that might seem anathema to us on the outside when talking about an organization that celebrates 1s and 0s. "*Free* 1s and 0s: that's what we want," is what a hacker club regular living in Toronto told me. "Free as in *unencumbered*, not the antonym of expensive," she added, reminding me also about how her club rejects what she later referred to as the "Google ethos"—a reference to a company that makes billions on algorithms that are as secretive and secure as nuclear launch codes.

"Free" for hackers means something quite different from what it does for Google execs.

You learned earlier how those 1s and 0s, especially when housed in a piece of "smart" farming equipment, are far from free and even further from freeing. And yet, there is a lot of talk about how precision farm equipment and Big Data are revolutionizing agriculture, in a good way, we're assured. I am not convinced that this promise squares with reality. Who is really profiting from this revolution? Eaters? Farmers? Nope. Companies? Bingo.

Monsanto has an uncanny knack of being able to identify the next "big thing" in agriculture. There is no crystal ball at company headquarters in Saint Louis, Missouri, I assure you. This knack is all about power: market power, to be precise. When you control as much of the input sector as this company does, you get to dictate what the next big thing is by your investments—a case of the self-fulfilling prophecy.

The company was at the forefront of the petrochemical and biotech revolutions; not surprisingly, it made massive investments in these areas before they took off. It should come as no surprise, then, to learn that Monsanto is poised to profit massively when Big Data becomes the toast of the town in conventional agriculture circles, which it already has, thanks in no small part to the company's hard-fought acquisitions.

Monsanto moved early and deftly to position itself as an industry leader, and it has acquired numerous farm data analytic companies since 2012. For instance, it shelled out $930 million in 2012 to acquire the Climate Corporation, which produces a popular software platform that enables farmers to practice so-called precision agriculture. The package gives users access to algorithms that show historical trends of soil moisture and crop level weather patterns going back thirty years. The product allows farmers to plug in different seed and receive an estimate, before planting season has even started, of their likely yields that fall. I have had farmers liken the technology to a crystal ball, though, as with the seeing-stones (the palantíri) in *The Lord of the Rings*, possession comes with risks.

Monsanto has stated that its Climate Pro sensors on harvesting equipment generate roughly seven gigabytes of data per acre. The United States has close to 100 million acres of corn in cultivation and another 80 million acres of soybeans. Do the math. That is a lot of data to be potentially entrusted to the company.

Of course, *who* owns all that data is a tricky question to answer. When you ask industry insiders, they will shoot back, without hesitation, "The farmers." Regardless of whether or not that is true, they know the ramifications of being anything but definitive about the point. Their market share depends on farmers at least believing Big Ag will not swoop in and snoop in on their farm. Farmers are understandably anxious about the subject. According to a recent report by the American Farm Bureau Federation, nearly three-fourths of the farmers surveyed said they were concerned that "others could use their information for commodity market speculation without their consent," and more than eight of every ten admitted to having no idea what the companies were doing with their data.[10]

Their concern appears warranted, at least according to some legal professionals. "While the raw data belong to farmers, the second it gets run through a proprietary algorithm, which is where the real magic happens, it enters a gray area," to quote one attorney who specializes in these issues. This is exactly why farm hackers fight to make data that are free, algorithms included, so as to eliminate even the possibility of a legal gray area.

Among the hackers I spoke with, access is more than a procedural artifact. For them, it was not enough simply to be legally allowed to tinker with a tractor's code. True access requires *capabilities*, such as the know-how to access code and then to do something meaningful with it. While the exemption to the Digital Millennium Copyright Act of 1998, or DMCA (mentioned in chapter 1), legally allows owners—but *only* owners—to tinker with their tractors' code, the fact that most lack the know-how to do this makes the exemption, for all practical purposes, meaningless.

I learned about Allen and his device through a Google search—the search engine might not be freeing, but I cannot deny its usefulness. I was curious about all the homemade "farmbots" out there, pieces of "smart" gardening technology that direct equipment to expel seed, water, and fertilizer in precise amounts. Allen had developed his own and was devoted to sharing it with the world.

Allen had been cutting wood before I arrived. Sitting in the kitchen of his house outside Flagstaff, Arizona, I noticed a mix of cool mountain air, wood, and two-cycle engine exhaust exuding from his clothes. A self-proclaimed "hacker foodie," Allen had constructed a "bot" for gardeners, which he described as a "complete garden monitoring and automation system, a digital green thumb for those not born with one." Like others I had seen, Allen's system allowed users to monitor various elements of their garden, from soil moisture to sunlight, temperature, precipitation, soil nutrient levels, and water drainage. Unlike those others, Allen's bot is built by users themselves, thanks to detailed instructions available online through various forums, though he was quick to deflect recognition, claiming it all to be the result of a community effort.

Allen was critical not only of firms that work with zeal to "enclose" what he called the "knowledge commons"—a reference to the legal process in England, and its colonies, of enclosing communal landholdings, thus restricting access to the proper owners. He also seemed equally frustrated with how food activists often think and talk about technology: "critically, as if there were only one way to farm, assuming Amish mores toward machines and the digital age."

This critique, he pointed out to me more than once, lumps corporate control with technology itself. We know that corporate control in conventional foodscapes is a huge problem. We also know that technology—*fossil fuel dependent* technology, no less—has historically displaced labor and made wholly unsustainable farming practices possible. But to say technology itself is the problem? Allen wasn't having any of it.

"There's this misconception that all of us looking to change our food system are a bunch of Luddites." Changing his speaking style, he imitated the detractors: "Oh, they're against bioengineered seed and genetically modified animals; they're against *all* technology." Back to his original voice, he continued, "We're not against technology"—"we" being fellow hackers. "What we're against is technology that makes you dependent on someone else."

Open source farmbots and farm hacker clubs illustrate an under-appreciated collaborative resistance against the highly proprietary revolution currently under way in conventional foodscapes. As I mentioned earlier, farmers are the original do-it-yourselfers, and a lot of them are eager to expand their fix-it expertise to include digital technologies, code included. I was struck, for instance, by how many farmers and gardeners knew what an Arduino board is—not exactly a lot of them, but more than a few. (For those unfamiliar with this piece of hardware, it is a microcontroller board used in open source applications. It also happened to be the brains of Allen's bot.) Relatedly, there was a strong desire among farmers, both big and small, to share this know-how so farmers could once again become DIYers when it comes to smart farm equipment, even commercial equipment.

Before we parted ways, Allen made a few phone calls. He was trying to get me some details about a hacker club meeting to be held in San Francisco the following week. I had mentioned that I would be in the Bay Area, and he brought up this group, which met twice a month, every first and third Tuesday, and generously offered to put me in contact with some of its members. I left Allen's house with a newfound appreciation for Arduino boards and the phone number of a new hacker contact living in Oakland, California, whom I called that night from my hotel room to set up a meeting for the following week.

Fast-forward six days . . .

It was not until entering the building that I learned it housed a software firm. The environment gave the evening a distinctly techy feel. It was a very inorganic experience, which was curious, given that we were talking about agriculture. That is not to say it was cold. Quite the opposite, in fact, thanks its convivial, warm, and inviting atmosphere.

The agenda for the evening, beginning at 6:00 p.m. and expressed using the twenty-four-hour system, was broken up as follows: 18:00–18:30, networking; 18:30–18:45, introductions; 18:45–20:45, hacking; 20:45–21:00, group share accomplishments. During "hacking" time, participants could self-select into any number of groups: compilation of plant growing information; planting software; vertical farming automation software; aeroponics; and hydroponics, to name a few.

What struck me most about this space was just how arbitrary separations are between "high" and "low" technology—a realization that ought to give us pause when resorting to dogmas about how new technologies are inferior to old ones, or vice versa. Seed, Arduino boards, and USB cables are technologies best learned in the company of others: material artifacts that cannot function fully, and *freely*, without attention to sharing know-how.

At one point during the hacker club meeting, Julie, one of the organizers, helped me properly solder pin headers to a microcontroller. "You see, it's like this," she told me as the scent of burning solder filled our nostrils. It took a light touch, which she communicated to me by first resting her hand on mine. I did eventually get the hang of it. But I remember thinking how glad I was to have someone literally hold my hand through the learning process. It was not a task I would have mastered as quickly by watching an instructional video on YouTube.

I had a lot of encounters like that during those three hours. Some involved the *smell* of solder, others the *feel* of a stable, well-constructed hydroponic stackable system, still others the *look* of blue-red-pink-purple-effect LED indoor grow lights when properly positioned above one's plants. The experience involved technologies that were perfectly legal and widely available. I daresay many were even inexpensive. Even so, this *access* did not result in my being able to put any of them to work, at least not before that night.

"It's about the conditions in which technology is born." Those were Julie's parting words, prior to our goodbyes, which in this case involved a hug and her giving me my very own Raspberry Pi 3 64-bit processor. She didn't say any more. But then again, she did not need to. I saw and felt it; heck, I even smelled it—the nose pinching, ironlike smell of solder is not soon forgotten.

Sharing has to be more than making sure others have access to stuff. Without the requisite knowledge that allows that stuff to be put to work, what good is it? Practicing technology and therefore playing a role in making it, especially in the presence of others, helps ensure against an "access" predicated on technologies that hoover wealth, when what they should be doing is dispersing it.

CHAPTER 6
Overcoming Barriers

We've talked about agricultural technologies and land—but ladders? The following is taken from a 1919 article titled "The Agricultural Ladder":

> The first rung of the agricultural ladder is represented by the period during which the embryo farmer is learning the rudiments of his trade. In the majority of cases this period is spent as an unpaid laborer on the home farm.
>
> The hired man stands on the second rung, the tenant on the third, while the farm owner has attained the fourth or final rung of the ladder.[1]

"The Agricultural Ladder" sought to describe the pathway to becoming a full-fledged owner-operator. Each rung represented a step closer to independence: unpaid family work (i.e., "doing chores"), wage labor, tenant operation, and, finally, full ownership. I admit some of the language in the century-old quote pains contemporary sensibilities— hired *man*: enough said. There is also that bit of strained analogous reasoning—*embryo* farmer: as if the "steps" reflect a preordained progression. All that aside, there is some truth to the outline. Every one of my high school friends who now farm followed this path.

Not that it applies, or has applied, in every case. In certain farming systems, the "ladder" is a rungless one. Think landless laborers in *The Grapes of Wrath*, which coincidently is set just a few years after "The Agricultural Ladder" was published—they had no hope of going anywhere.[2] It is also worth noting that the metaphor not-too-subtly perpetuates the Jeffersonian ideal, with ownership representing the crowning achievement of agrarian social mobility.

It would not surprise me if you had not heard the term before. The metaphor is not used much these days, in large part because the top rungs are closed to most people.

My interest in the ladder lies in something implied in the progression from step to step. Knowing *how to* farm is as real a barrier to agriculture as *finding a* farm, and in some ways it is even more of one. Say we make farmland accessible to the nonfarmers who dream of taking up this profession. What then? What does that solve if those well intentioned people lack a working knowledge of the life they now find themselves in?

How did farmers historically learn their profession? Not from a textbook. Picture it: the famed Grant Wood painting *American Gothic*, substituting the pitchfork in the gentleman's hand for a book titled *How to Farm*.

"Farming isn't like accounting," I remember one farmer telling me. It was not meant as a dig to accountants. He was simply stating a fact about how one learns to farm. Farmers learn to farm by . . . wait for it: *farming*.[3]

Growing up on a farm and climbing "up" the agricultural ladder: that is how individuals, for generations, learned to farm, especially in areas such as the Midwest. Granted, some of my farming friends from high school went off to college before coming back to agriculture. Most went to Iowa State University, my home state's land grant institution. There they enrolled in agriculture related classes, subjects ranging from weed science to agricultural economics, plant genetics, and agronomy. Even a degree in agricultural science—an actual major at some land grants— does not teach you to be farmer, no more than a degree in aeronautical science teaches you to be a pilot.

Which is why I am worried. From a production standpoint, conventional foodscapes have been largely self-regenerative, thanks to the agricultural ladder. Alternative foodscapes, meanwhile, do not have that inborn tendency toward mimicry. Many of these growers are first-generation, first-time farmers.[4] If we want alternatives to thrive, we have to get serious about giving people the experience of farming, to attract them to the profession and then to teach them about it.

Historically, institutions have played an important role in helping farmers acquire both land and knowledge. The federal government has a long history of facilitating land transfer, starting with the Homestead Act of 1862. Its role today is far more muted, confined to offering reduced interest loans. Public universities, meanwhile, traditionally communicated a certain type of knowledge, namely, about fertilizer, feed, and irrigation schedules, business acumen, and the like. The farm family, meanwhile, was left with the unsung task of conveying everything else, imparting to future farmers all the hands-on knowledge needed to run a successful operation.

It is time to revisit that division of labor.

The concept of the agricultural ladder describes less and less the processes by which people get into farming. A recent survey conducted in Canada found that among those who reported farming for fewer than five years, only 30 percent claimed to be from family farm backgrounds, while 60 percent had nonagricultural backgrounds. Meanwhile, the majority of those who had been farming for more than ten years reported having been raised on a farm.[5]

With the stage set, I wish to introduce Doris, a first-generation beginning farmer in Northern California. Doris is part of the Farmers Guild community. The Farmers Guild is a collection of ten local guilds located throughout Northern California that individually serve their communities and partner organizations. The Farmers Guild's website explains:

> We are the newest wave of farmers, ranchers, and sustainable food system advocates. With a passion for feeding our local communities, we unite to share skills, knowledge and a meal after a day in the field. Founded by farmers for farmers, we support healthy food production by collectively striving toward the economic viability of agriculture as well as the social networks to attract, cultivate and sustain a new generation ready to work the land.[6]

"Guild": generally defined as an association of people with similar interests or pursuits, typically associated with craftsmen and craftswomen. I especially like the term because of its historical association with trades and crafts, which further implies a skill that one has to *do* to learn— that's the whole rationale for apprenticeships. This explains the group's emphasis on sharing. Note that the term "share" makes an appearance in the above block quote *before* the reference to economic viability. Compare this with, for instance, the Iowa Corn Growers Association's mission statement, which in its first paragraph pledges "to create opportunities for long-term Iowa corn grower profitability."[7]

Doris and I wanted to find someplace quiet, so we walked to a grove of apple trees tucked behind the barn. Standing in the orchard, its canopies pregnant with blossoms drifting overhead, we talked about the Farmers Guild's role in sustaining alternative foodscapes through sharing.

She began by telling me what the federal government thinks about farm succession, noting that the Farm Service Agency—an agency of the

U.S. Department of Agriculture—provides loans for beginning farmers; it even sets money aside to target historically underserved populations. While serving all farmers and ranchers, the agency is required, by statute, to dedicate a portion of its loans to farmers and ranchers who fall in the following categories: women; African Americans; Alaskan Natives; American Indians; Hispanics; Asians; and Native Hawaiians and Pacific Islanders.[8]

Doris continued: "I'm not saying it's easy to get your hands on affordable land, especially here in California. But while there are institutions and government entities tasked with making land more accessible, there's no government program tasked with helping people learn to farm once they get the land."

Looking up at an aircraft flying overhead, its contrails like delicate white threads stitching together the billowy clouds that were decorating the sky, she added, "What good is land if you don't know what to do with it?"

The Farmers Guild averages a little more than an event per month, though this average hides considerable variability; some times of the year are certainly busier than others. I talked with Doris in early April, at a gathering on compost production and application and seed germination and plant transplanting.

Explaining these lulls in the Guild's event schedule, Doris said, "Since we're about providing farmer-to-farmer hands-on knowledge, we generally hold events when there's something to do. The thing about peer-to-peer experiential learning is that you can't do it with handouts"—a reference to the ubiquitous brochures that were part of the long criticized extension model common in twentieth-century land grant universities.[9] In other words, farming knowledge cannot be explained but has to be experienced.

Another barrier is the well documented fact that agricultural social networks can be tricky nuts to crack if you are not white and male.[10]

Individuals identifying as white own well over 90 percent of all farmland nationally.[11] According to the USDA's 2012 Census of Agriculture, of the 2.1 million farmers in the United States, 67,000 were Hispanic (3 percent of all farmers); almost 38,000 were American Indian (1.8 percent of the total); more than 33,000 were black (1.5 percent of the total); and nearly 14,000 were Asian (0.7 percent of the total).[12] As for the gender breakdown, 14 percent of principal operators were female.

Doris again, talking about her participation in the California Farm Bureau Federation's Young Farmers and Ranchers Conference: "As a woman at a more conventional farm networking event, I don't always feel like I belong." The Farm Bureau Federation is widely considered to be a fairly conservative, conventional farm lobbying organization. It wasn't until 2015, for example, that it admitted publicly that climate change was real. Doris talked freely about how being a woman has caused consternation when she is navigating these conventional networks. "People don't know what to do with me," she explained with a smile and a slightly uplifted chin—the look of pride. Doris was raised in the Los Angeles suburbs. "Then they find out I don't have a farming background. That's strike two. I'm not taken seriously from that point on."

Others repeated Doris's comments. I had the opportunity to talk with multiple female operators who were part of the Farmers Guild community. The event I was participating in had more women in attendance than men, which in itself was telling. I have been to enough "field days" in the Midwest, sponsored by the likes of Pioneer Seed and Monsanto, to know how male-centric conventional farm networks can look.

I met one of those women knee-deep in shit. No symbolism implied. I had not unintentionally put my foot in my mouth or anything like that. I was actually standing in poop, or at least what used to be poop—again, the Guild event I had attended was about compost.

Mary and I talked at length about what the Farmers Guild is and what it means to those who are a part of it. Turning manure over with a shovel, she explained: "We're more than the sum of our parts—like this compost—which is what makes us unique from traditional farming associations." Struck by this assertion, I asked for clarification. (Whenever a group compares itself to compost, you always ask for clarification.) After ramming the head of the shovel into the ground below our feet, she placed both hands on the handle. It looked like she was getting comfortable.

"It's the Horatio Alger myth—that pull-yourself-up-by-your-boot-straps crap. It runs deep in agriculture." Alger, a novelist who wrote tales about impoverished young men overcoming adversity, helped popularize the rags-to-riches story line in the late 1880s. Mary added, mockingly, "Good farmers don't need anyone else." Back in her regular voice, she said, "That's where we go wrong; farmers are taught to be independent and autonomous, *to a fault.*"

There is actually a good bit of research backing up Mary's depiction, what one scholar has identified as the ideology of individualism within agriculture.[13] I did not see evidence of this ideology—that "pull-yourself-up-by-your-bootstraps crap"—at the Farmers Guild. Mary again: "Here, we appreciate that interdependence isn't a sign of weakness but a strategy for greater independence."

Mary was saying, as I understood her, that in conventional farming circles, you are socialized to not rely on others. It is worth noting that this ideology is often blamed for skyrocketing rates of depression and suicide among farming men, percentages that greatly exceed those for male populations in urban areas.[14] To believe that success means not having to ask for help is not only problematic from the perspective of community building and integration; it can also make you sick, both physically and mentally.

The Farmers Guild network sees *inter*dependence as requisite for independence and, ultimately, well-being. This also brings us back to the compost analogy, about how this community is more than the sum of its parts.

My conversation with Mary concluded at the machine shed as we returned our shovels, gloves, and boots. "Look at how we share genetic stocks and the knowledge that goes along with them." She was telling me about all the things that members of the group reciprocate, from expertise and stories to seeds and animals. "Farmers are at the mercy of large companies. To say those farmers back in Iowa"—we had just finished discussing a seed corn field day I had recently attended in the Hawkeye State—"are independent, *really* independent, goes against the facts." Her point—that most conventional farmers are stuck between a rock (the companies they buy inputs from) and a hard place (those they sell their commodities to)—is a common theme of this book.

After handshakes and promises to stay in touch, Mary left me with this parting comment: "Farmers Guild offers a lifeline to beginning and even lifelong farmers." Regardless of the metaphor—*lifeline* or *ladder*—the key point of both is that aspiring farmers need to be part of a knowledge community.

Chicago's Michigan Avenue in December is a magical place: ice-skating in Millennium Park, the more than seventy-five-year-old *Christmas around the World* exhibit at the Museum of Science and Industry, and colorful storefront displays. It is a Magnificent Mile, well deserving of the name. I never turn down an opportunity to return to the city, especially at this time of year.

The opportunity, in this particular case, was an invitation by officers of the Federal Reserve Bank of Chicago. They were helping plan a workshop on what they were calling the "circular economy" and thought it might help to throw a social scientist into the mix. They were also interested in hearing about the findings involving a study of producer and consumer food cooperatives in Colorado that I was wrapping up. The workshop itself is not relevant to this story. I am telling you about it as a means of introducing Julia.

Have you ever looked at someone and sworn they were brighter than everyone else, like the lead in a theatrical production constantly illuminated by a giant unseen light source? Have you ever seen someone walk with such energy that it looked like they were skipping? Have you ever seen someone's entire body coil like a spring before meeting another for the first time and watched their facial expressions explode the instant they did? Have you ever met someone with the power to reduce the background noise of a room by simply talking?

Julia was a singularity: a point where the laws of physics seemed to break down. Of course she was flesh and blood. But her ability to command a room: I hadn't seen anyone with such an ability without assistance from a title—Mr. President, Madame Secretary, Your Majesty.

A community activist residing in Chicago's South Side, Julia had spent the better part of thirty years "fighting," in her words, "to do right for her community." That fight was on full display at the workshop, as when she berated city officials—the room was full of them, making the image particularly unforgettable—for their aggressive wooing of Walmart. "As if *that* will solve food insecurity in our city," she claimed, rather loudly. Shortly after, once the scattering of applause from audience members had stopped, she added, "You can't have community development without community. What we don't need are policies that gut our communities and make collaboration even more difficult."

Afterward I approached, wanting to learn more about her and her community's struggles. Julia launched into a remarkable story about overcoming numerous barriers.

How? One word: *cooperation.*

Twenty-four hours later, we were sitting in the parking lot of a formerly abandoned shopping center. I was eagerly waiting to tour a more than 10,000-square-foot grocery store: a business proudly envisioned, owned, and operated by some seven hundred members of the surrounding community. "You're looking at what's possible with grassroots blood, sweat, and tears," Julia told me. And money, I later learned—loans and grants, totaling more than $2 million, had financed the cooperative's opening.

Riding to this site, I learned about its recent past. Julia provided the history lesson as she drove. You would have thought she could see the road from her smartphone, given how often her eyes were on that screen rather than on the analog windshield that most of use to navigate the road. A year ago, she said, I would have been driving through a USDA defined food desert. Half the households had been food insecure before the co-op opened.

First impressions were all positive. There was a bus stop next to the parking lot and another a half block away. I also remember being surprised by what I did *not* see: orphaned shopping carts. All were sitting securely in assigned return receptacles. This was unlike the scene at the chain store where I'd been the day before. Its lot had been littered with carts taking up parking spaces, most of them two wheels up against a tree island. People have actually studied this behavior, arguing that it can indicate, among other things, a lack of commitment to the establishment.[15] When you care about something, you tend to take care of it. When was the last time you washed a rental car?

As I approached the co-op's automatic sliding doors, my eyes went to the oversized sale signs plastered across the building's lower front facade. Walking into the store, I grabbed a flyer listing "deals for the week." Deli meat: $3.00 per pound. Whole chickens: $0.80 per pound. Bananas: $0.50 per pound. Those prices rival anything the chains can offer.

Looking up from the flyer, I saw Julia moving ahead, now halfway to the back of the store. She seemed to float down the aisle. Running to catch up, I found her leaning against the meat case. "Michael, I'd like to introduce you to our in-house butcher."

In most stores, this profession has gone the way of the blacksmith. It is far cheaper for stores to buy case-ready meat that has been cut and packaged in a centralized facility. Not here. I asked about this oddity. Julia and the butcher, a thirty-two-year-old woman who had emigrated to the United States from Ukraine as a toddler with her parents, exchanged a look. The butcher, Anastasia, turned in my direction. Her expression projected pride, while her tone of voice had a hint of defensiveness to it. She answered matter-of-factly: "We're a cooperative, which means we have the benefit of not having to think only about the bottom line. We have to always ask ourselves 'What does the community want?' when making business decisions."

Julia moved around the counter and put her arm around Anastasia, giving her an open faced hug, and chimed in. "In this case, we know what the community wants because they're co-owners. And they want to know who's cutting their meat."

This also explains why and how the cooperative is able to pay its employees at least $14.00 per hour. This is more than the citywide $10.50 per hour minimum wage, and more than the $13.00 hourly rate set to take effect in 2019 thanks to a 2014 city ordinance. Why? Because doing so is important to members.

Lo and behold, it also proved a wise business move. Julia was quick to mention how this better-than-average wage had reduced worker turnover and improved customer service. "It's all connected," Julia reminded me in a somewhat scolding tone, as if she were talking to a skeptic. "You treat your workers like shit, they're going to treat customers like shit, not like their jobs, and leave the moment something better comes along. And your customers aren't going to be too happy, either"—my mind immediately went back to those full shopping cart receptacles.

In the world of tight margins that is food retail, even big chains— we're talking about the Krogers and Walmarts of the sector: the Big Dogs—are actually exploring the idea of paying their workers more, a rare instance of the business community being more progressive than many politicians, even those claiming to be pro-business. The move, at its face, might seem counterintuitive until you realize the long-term savings that come with treating workers like something other than cogs in a machine.

The community has eliminated its food desert designation. It was also a social capital desert and thus a knowledge exchange desert. Not any longer.

It did not take long for me to realize that the cooperative was improving food access within the community. As for understanding the positive impact it was having on sharing knowledge? That took the rest of the afternoon to figure out.

After a tour of the retail space, Julia took me to the rear of the store and handed me off to Nicole, one of the cooperative's assistant managers. "We hold classes here at least once a week," she explained as we entered a room that reminded me of a model kitchen you might see on display at Lowe's. (I was close. It had been donated by a local home builder—a kitchen from one of the model homes.) Handing me a calendar that listed upcoming and recent events, Nicole added, "We take our self-imposed charge of doing things that benefit our community seriously. We also realize that while plopping a grocery store in a food desert is a positive first step, it isn't the be-all and end-all to the problem."

As I stood there looking around, I had time to take in my surroundings. The air in the room smelled of sage and rosemary chicken and what I initially thought was pie, either cherry or cherry apple. Casting my gaze around, I spotted a roaster, one of those big ones you might see at a family reunion, and, resting by the sink, a large pan of cherry crisp. Seeing my eyes fall upon the food, Nicole volunteered, as if she could read my mind, and my stomach, "For tonight—a board meeting."

Stepping between the sink and me, Nicole went on to tell me about the cooking classes offered regularly by the cooperative. What struck me about her description was not that there were classes, or even that they were free. As nutritional literature campaigns have grown in popularity, so has the realization that people lack basic cooking skills to put that newfound nutritional knowledge to work. But these classes weren't just about teaching people to cook.

Members of the community sign up to be an "instructor for a day." Nicole handed me a bright yellow flyer with large lettering at the top: "Learn About a Culturally Significant Dish!" A little farther down, "Bean and plantain pottage"—a traditional Nigerian dish, Nicole informed me.

At an earlier event, attendees had been treated to a lesson on tamales. This was not your typical cooking class. I remember thinking, *If HGTV aired cooking shows like this, I might actually watch!* Yes, participants learned how to make this Mexican staple. But in addition, the instructor went to great lengths to explain the cultural significance of the dish. Corn and its place in understanding Mexican heritage: where does one begin? As Nicole put it, "Everyone left that event with a newfound appreciation for our neighbors to the south." If only everyone took such a class, especially those wanting to wall themselves off from this nation and its people.

"What better way to break down cultural barriers, to give people an appreciation for others different from themselves, than through food?" Nicole's excitement was infectious. Her face lit up while her arms moved up and down to give her words added weight. The effect created the gestalt of a human lightning bug.

Nicole bent down behind the island. After a few seconds of rustling around, she emerged with a three-ring binder. Opening it, she read off the names and self-identified ethnicities of recent instructors: Vietnamese, Korean, African American, Jamaican, German, Mexican, Kenyan, and Polish, to name the ones I managed to record.

Nicole then unfolded a property map of the surrounding community and spread it on the countertop.

"Why are some properties distinguished with a yellow highlighter mark?," I asked.

Those who participate in the cooking class have their houses marked on the map, I was told. "It's a way to make sure we're serving the whole community and not just pockets of it." Mission accomplished, given that yellow dots covered the map.

I then noticed tick marks next to most of the yellow dots. "Repeat customers." Not only were these marks evenly distributed across the map, but there were also a lot of them.

It is hard to know just how deeply these experiences affected participants, especially from the standpoint of creating cultural competencies. But given the United States' general cultural incompetence, we need all the help we can get. Did you see that Gallup study from 2016? The best predictor of whether individuals support things like building a wall between the United States and Mexico and who believe nonwhites have not contributed as much to civilization as those of European descent is how white their social networks are.[16]

Before escorting me back into the store and reuniting me with Julia, Nicole offered some parting words. The conversation had veered to how "sharing" is polysemous, that it has multiple meanings. Nicole was keen to distinguish between what Uber facilitates and what I was being shown that day in Chicago's South Side.

"If this," she said—both arms out and head tilting subtly to the left, then to the right—"isn't getting people to exchange stories, culturally specific knowledge, worldviews, then it's failing as a sharing platform. If we can better understand each other by sharing time, knowledge, and experiences, the other stuff will work itself out. Markets are unfair because people are. Ignorance is our problem."

Whoever said good fences make good neighbors never visited this cooperative.

CHAPTER 7

Walls Make Terrible Neighbors

At one point during her widely viewed Ted Talk, Rachel Botsman, author of *What's Mine Is Yours: The Rise of Collaborative Consumption*, asked the audience for a show of hands from those who owned a power drill. Nearly everyone lifted a palm.[1] "It's kind of ridiculous, isn't it?" she said, with a mix of disbelief and sadness, "because what you need is the hole, not the drill." Pausing to let her point sink in—*because what you need is the hole, not the drill*—she then swooped in with the solution. "Why don't you rent the drill? Or rent out your own drill to other people and make some money from it?"

The idea of collaborative consumption, and the drill meme, grew legs and took on a life of its own, at least in media channels. The *Guardian*, *Entrepreneur* magazine, *Time*, the *New York Daily News*, the *New York Times*, and *Wired* all had articles touting peer-to-peer renting, with the venerable drill acting as a trope for something quite profound—a revolution. To quote Brian Chesky, the cofounder and CEO of Airbnb, "There are 80 million power drills in America that are used an average of 13 minutes. Does everyone really need their own drill?"[2]

The idea did and does make sense. It's brilliant, actually. There's just one little problem, a hiccup keeping us from swallowing the thing whole. Adam Berk, the founder of Neighborrow, put his finger on it when he said, "Everything made sense except that nobody gives a shit."[3]

It is a good point, if you can look past the profanity and absolute thinking. Sharing does have its virtues. So why not do more of it?

Camila, a hairstylist living in Queens, had been in the New York City metro area for the past twelve months. Prior to that, she had spent her entire life in Bogotá, Colombia. Our encounter was both personal and professional. Personal: I was hungry and wanted to eat some home cooked Colombian cuisine. Professional: I had learned about Camila and her business, supported by the AirDine app, through friends, and I wanted to talk with her and some of her customers.

I have mentioned meal sharing repeatedly—at the risk of giving the impression that such platforms play a significant role in feeding people, especially urban hipsters and foodies. They do not. Talking with aspiring chefs, eaters, and industry insiders has taught me that the challenges faced by the likes of AirDine have less to do with finding cooks who are willing to invite total strangers into their homes. The greatest obstacle is finding people willing to go to a total stranger's house to eat.

Camila's enthusiasm for cooking and being able to share it with others was obvious within seconds of my stepping into her narrow entryway. I was led to her cooking and dining area and noticed immediately the tile, which was more backdrop than backsplash, as it covered nearly the entire wall. Crimson red tiles. The lighting from above gave the effect of the room being on fire.

In her thick Colombian accent, accompanied by conspicuous hand gestures, Camila spoke more than once of how she loved being an AirDine host. "I was 100 percent behind the idea the moment I first learned about it. I love to piddle in the kitchen, but I live alone. Having someone to cook for allows me to do what I wouldn't otherwise be able to do: cook and eat with others!" She clapped her hands together in front of her face with the word "others."

Like most hosts I spoke with, Camila also admitted that guests were not exactly knocking down her door to eat, though she did have some devoted followers. "I'll get about one a week, which surprises me. Did you see all the restaurants around here?" I had. You could not visit Camila's apartment without passing two or three within a two-block radius, regardless of the direction of your approach.

Others have similarly commented on eaters' initial reluctance to participate in these platforms, from hosts to angel investors with ownership equity. When asked to explain this apparent lack of demand, often in cities where eating out has become as commonplace as using Uber, the answers I got were mixed. Some pointed out that the hosts are the ones in control of the situation. They have home field advantage. It is their house, after all. For eaters it feels like, well, going to a complete stranger's place to eat, which is not something we are used to doing.

One individual, an investor, put this advantage in the following colorful—if dark hues are a color—way: "You might be going to the home of an ax murderer; at least when you are a host, if your guest does turn out to be a deranged killer, you can take comfort in knowing the location of your knives. Heck, you'll be holding one some of the time while you're cooking."

Others speculated that not knowing more about how the food is being prepared might turn away some eaters, creating anxiety over whether their meal is actually safe to eat. Camila made reference to this at one point in the evening, *after* we had eaten, I noticed. Rolling the fat end of her upright port glass between her palms, she explained, "Cooks know how their food was prepared; they made it, so they should trust that it's safe to eat. Guests, on the other hand, almost have to take it on faith that they're eating something that won't get them sick."

Having come from Colombia, Camila also thought that some of the barriers to the business are cultural. With the port glass now resting on the table, freeing her hands to animate and accentuate her points, she continued: "I was raised thinking it was perfectly normal to open your house to people. Then"—*bam!*, both hands slapped the tabletop—"I came to America and learned quickly that not everyone thinks and eats that way."

While seemingly unconnected, these two points, about control and culture, are closely related. The connecting thread: social distance. We generally do not talk, let alone eat, with people all that different from us anymore. And as for strangers: we all know what we teach our kids at a young age about them. Not that the advice doesn't have its merits. But those merits come with costs, too.

Camila made the connection, noting the cultural differences between what she knew in her country of birth and those she has experienced in the United States. At one point in our conversation, right after the *bandeja paisa* had been served, she quipped, "For such a free country, you sure seem afraid to interact with people you don't know."

Camila would have surely disapproved of the aforementioned "ax murderer" remark. That *that* would be the first thing to pop into someone's mind when contemplating eating at another's house says something about the state of things. Rather than worrying about not having anything to talk about—or *a million other things*—their mind goes there?

The social friction rubbing political discourse raw today, where some think it is okay to publicly call Mexicans rapists and where we are quick to associate strangers with ax murders, also colors concerns over food safety when it comes to peer-to-peer food sharing. Camila was trying to make precisely this point. This is not to suggest that Americans recoil at the thought of eating at another person's house. We might have our concerns—such as when I attend family reunions in the summer and see potato salad sitting for hours under the hot sun. Yet we generally keep those concerns to ourselves, for the sake of keeping the peace, while at the same time silently making sure to steer away from anything questionable.

I am not suggesting that eating at a stranger's home is risk free. But something is socially amiss when the default position becomes *strangers and their food cannot be trusted*, even though, I should add, these meal sharing platforms monitor their chefs' cooking spaces. Meal sharing businesses, at least the ones I am familiar with, always have someone come and inspect prospective chefs' kitchens before they are admitted to their "team." Skirting city or state health inspectors, as some of these platforms do, does not mean their chefs skirt common sense. These platforms generally require some level of food safety training, which is more than I can say about, say, Uber Eats, an online platform for meal ordering and delivery—meal handling comes with risks too, let's not forget.

In Colombia, Camila was raised to give people the benefit of the doubt when it came to eating at their home. "You just trust them," is how she blithely put it. The risk of that position, of course, is illness: an upset stomach, perhaps some diarrhea, and, yes, maybe even death. These are real risks, to be sure. But those risks are no different from those you incur when you eat at the house of a friend or family member. Why the double standard?

I have already given the answer. Social distance. It is hard to give strangers the benefit of doubt if we are worried about them being ax murderers.

Worrying about whether a host might be harboring a killer in the kitchen—perhaps *E. coli* lurking on the counter—is not even the worst of it. As Camila explained, having brown skin and a "Spanish sounding surname" has forced her to confront those lesser angels that have taken control of a small but vocal percentage of our electorate.

With her normally "vocal" arms and hands lying silent, Camila looked at me. The pain in her voice gave her words more weight than any physical gesture could. "Being from south of the border has cost me." She then told me about an instance in which she had received feedback for a meal she never served: vile comments that centered on her ethnicity and questioned her legal right to live in the country. "A hit-and-run job," based solely on information contained in her profile, was how she explained the written attack.

At that moment, her hands came back to life. Not the exaggerated movements that I had grown accustomed to seeing: something else, not at all animated by excitement or pleasure. Shaking.

"There are so many people today who think the only good Muslim is a dead Muslim, who hate people from Mexico and Central and South America, and African Americans too. The risk for bigots using something like AirDine has nothing to do with food safety. The risk lies in going to someone's house and being greeted at the door by brown skin or by someone wearing a turban."

It is an interesting, and in equal parts sad, question: how much of this social resistance to peer-to-peer meal sharing is about fears over food safety and how much is about *fear, period*? I kept my ears open from that point on for similar experiences among meal sharing hosts, especially those with dark skin or non–Anglo sounding surnames. Regrettably, Camila's was not the only story animated by racism, ignorance, and fear.

How we can overcome those obstacles, through sharing, no less, is the subject of this and the remaining chapters.

The stories I have been telling, while informed by first-person accounts, are plucked from a single, fixed point. There is nothing wrong with this approach. Journalists, politicians, social scientists—heck, everyone—makes conclusions and tells stories based on one-off encounters. I am not questioning this practice. Let's also be realistic. It is hard enough getting people to make time in their busy lives to have someone like me intrude and ask a bunch of questions. To do that twice—that is a bridge too far for all but the most patient.

When presented, however, with the opportunity to talk to someone twice, you treat it as Yogi Berra told us to treat a fork in the road. You take it.

I was introduced to Catherine, a commercial real estate agent, through a mutual friend. She had been in Colorado only a month, having moved to Denver with her husband and daughter. She had come from a suburb of Chicago—the neighborhood, a gated community. Catherine described wanting to become part of her new community, which is what attracted her to a local food cooperative. "We've always been active in our community; we want that same feeling here," was how she explained it. That "community" back in Chicagoland sounded quite exclusive, involving membership in a posh country club, the Commercial Club of Chicago (I had to do an Internet search on that one; it's an elite club, founded in 1877), and PTA committees in their child's private school. The community she had left was a monoculture: almost all white, exclusively affluent, and mostly right of center in its politics.

Catherine seemed to be on track to reproduce what she'd had, and who she had been, while living in Chicago. She and her husband picked the community that they did in part because of its country club—"one of the best in the state," she exclaimed proudly. As for the new neighborhood, while not gated, it might as well have been. The price of a neighboring house listed for sale made it clear that this was a place for One Percenters.

An urban food co-op membership was something entirely new for Catherine.

The demographics of the cooperative looked a lot like Catherine's household, if you include in that comparison the nanny, cleaning person, yard person, and fishpond person. Yes, a fishpond person: in front of the house was a kitchen table sized pond with a bridge you had to cross to reach the front door. "Your own moat," I said jokingly. Anecdotes aside, the co-op was *diverse*, socially, culturally, politically, and economically.

Having navigated the moat, I crossed the threshold and entered a large sitting room. Moments later, Catherine and I were seated comfortably in a room decorated with pieces of oversized plush furniture, their bulk amplified by throw pillows and blankets in an array of colors and fabrics. The décor gave the impression that the room would swallow anything louder than a whisper. I recall that as I sat down, there was an eruption of dust from the soft cushions, a type of nonvocal groan from something being put to work for the first time in days. Against the low early morning dawn, sun danced off particles that seemed suspended in space, carried by currents that I could not explain.

Most of that first meeting was spent discussing the co-op's most worthy and most challenging elements. For someone who had initially justified joining the co-op to become better integrated into the community, Catherine did not spent much time talking about people, other than her kids and husband. Squinting as the sunlight poked through a window behind me and aimed its rays at her now illuminated face, she told me the real reason why she had joined the co-op. Two kept creeping into the conversation, cost and nutrition, as when she explained that the value of her co-op membership resided principally in her ability to "get inexpensive fresh, locally sourced, wholesome food."

The challenges she faced, meanwhile, were significant. This inexpensive, wholesome food did come at a cost.

Catherine portrayed the volunteering assignments as "at times un-comfortable." This particular cooperative went beyond the pay-to-play model; it strongly encouraged members to volunteer as part of their "dues." These initial tasks took many forms, from working on the store floor to being on various committees and serving as a co-op ambassador, where you drum up support and members for the organization.

Catherine was coy when asked to explain what she meant by being uncomfortable. "I just don't have much in common with a lot of the people I work with," was the closest she came to providing an explanation. It was not until near the end of the interview, when I asked if she had any memorable stories involving a co-op experience, that I managed to get some insight into what not having "much in common" meant.

She recounted two stories. Each involved individuals with backgrounds and income brackets different from those in the community she'd left behind in Chicago. The specifics of both, while interesting, are secondary to the fact that Catherine's early anxiety about volunteering resided in her being made to interact with people whom she was not used to interacting with. In these accounts, she talked about "having to work with someone who spoke broken English." Her first story involved volunteering alongside an immigrant from Vietnam. In the second, the person had been born and raised in Nicaragua. Although Catherine mentioned specifically the language barrier, her words betrayed a deeper unease. At one point, she remarked, "I've interacted with immigrants but usually on an employer-employee basis." Which I took to mean *This is the first time I've had to interact with immigrants as social equals.*

Catherine's feelings were not unique. Scholars have reported similar findings in both controlled experimental designs and noncontrived social settings. Within a short time of meeting, people with greater status begin to disengage from conversations, as evidenced by less head nodding and laughing, when paired with someone "below" them in the social hierarchy.[4] If the conversation does continue, it likely devolves into a one-way talk, where those with greater status resort to nonengaged head nods as they scan the crowd for someone more worthy of their attention.[5] In a word, these exchanges tend to make those involved *uncomfortable.*

Fast-forward two years.

I reentered Catherine's life on a hot August day. Given the hundred-degree-plus temps, we decided it best to reconvene in the cool confines of her house. To say the room of our first meeting had undergone a makeover would not have done justice to the scope of change. "Reborn" might be a better term. Besides the cold, slick, and reflective leather that had replaced the warm, textured, and absorbing plush, the room had gotten taller. Soaring vaulted satin ceilings had replaced the orange-peel textured drywall that previously rested within jumping reach overhead. On entering the room, I was greeted by a chocolate dachshund—also new. His bark echoed through the room as if we were in the gymnasium at my son's elementary school.

Over iced coffees and chocolate chip cookies we discussed food, politics, and her cooperative experiences to date. At first blush, things looked much the same. Her real estate practice was thriving. She and her family were also making time to enjoy their country club membership. Catherine had even gotten her feet wet sloshing around in state politics by helping fundraise for local Republican candidates.

It was not until we delved into her comings, goings, and doings with the co-op that I was able to discern some meaningful differences in *this* Catherine compared with the one I had interviewed two years prior.

Catherine's participation in the cooperative had not waned. If anything, it appeared to have increased. By her account, she was "more involved in co-op politics and management now than ever." Her daughter, a teenager, had even started volunteering, serving on a committee charged with expanding outreach opportunities.

Recalling our first interview and the anxiety I had detected in some of Catherine's responses, I asked her to tell me about any especially memorable volunteer experiences. The resulting conversation was wide ranging and wandering. After two years, Catherine had done about anything and everything one could do as a volunteer—she'd done committee work and website design, served as checker and bagger and as house party host to get the word out about the co-op, stocked shelves, and picked up produce from local growers.

In contrast to our first interview, Catherine made no reference to language barriers. I found this especially striking, given that she continued to volunteer alongside diverse populations, including people who spoke English as a second, or even third, language. I wanted to hear especially about her experiences in working alongside co-op members who were different from her and her family—in other words, not white and most definitely not affluent. One particular exchange is worth recounting. It involved what she called an "outreach project to a Hispanic neighborhood."

About a year earlier, the co-op had made an intentional effort to engage more directly with surrounding disadvantaged neighborhoods and households in an attempt to, in Catherine's words, "do something about food security in the area." A predominately Hispanic community was located just miles away from the store, in a USDA defined food desert, no less. Cooperative members, some of whom called that neighborhood home, began engaging with households to learn about their food needs in the hope that the co-op could better serve them.

"I ended up on that committee in part because I had a large enough vehicle," Catherine recalled. The outreach committee was composed primarily of native Spanish speakers. It quickly became apparent that transportation was going to be a real barrier to participation. Catherine again: "Not everyone had a car, or at least a reliable one. No one had anything large enough to hold all of us. That's where I came into the picture, to help bus people around the neighborhood."

It was during this discussion that her past political activities, namely, as a partisan fundraiser, entered the picture. Holding a half-eaten cookie in her left hand, she told me how experiences with the cooperative had changed her attitudes toward immigrants. "If my friends back in Chicago could have seen me loading up my SUV with who I had in it." She was chuckling now, covering her mouth with the back of her right hand as she tried to finish chewing. "We weren't exactly bleeding hearts"—as in, progressive Democrats. Her hands returned to her lap, cookie and laughter both gone. "We were just the opposite." I noticed that she included herself in that group and that she used past tense. "Generally, we supported candidates who were all about being tough on crime, and that included being hard on those here illegally." Her voice got quieter, perhaps with regret.

I asked whether her attitudes had changed at all. She replied faintly, a wistful look in her eyes, admitting that her political beliefs "had evolved."

I'm always careful when broaching a person's politics, even more so in today's climate. I tried to navigate these waters delicately. In the end, Catherine identified issues such as immigration reform, poverty, and health care in which her beliefs had moved "closer to the center than where they were a few years back."

It was undoubtedly an interesting admission. But *why* had she changed her mind?

"There are two takeaways that I have from all those experiences," Catherine said, referring to her time with the cooperative and its members. "The first, it's easy to be hard on a population when you never have to interact with them." If only we all displayed this much self-reflectiveness and honesty. "And second, there is something distinct about the *cooperative* experience."

And here's where she brought up sharing. "There's something to be said about sharing a business, where you have a blurring of lines between producers and consumers, owners and workers." Just like that, unprompted, this registered Republication went there, talking about the virtues of a sharing economy. To justify this position, she started by talking about efficiencies, perhaps as much for her sake as for mine—for example, "There are labor efficiencies that come with avoiding worker turnover by having the owners do the work." This proved a short-lived volley, however, as the conversation quickly turned to the noneconomic virtues of working and owning together.

"At the end of the day, there's something even more valuable than money that these places are generating." Catherine was talking about cooperatives specifically, though I am sure she would be comfortable generalizing to any platform that meaningfully brought people from diverse backgrounds together. "Let's not forget, economies work best when people don't hate each other. So that ought to be priority number one: *community building*"—there was that intonation again.

With that, she stood and grabbed the now bare cookie plate. *Time's up*, I thought. Her daughter needed to be picked up from a friend's house. While walking to the kitchen, Catherine said over her shoulder, "I'm still a pretty traditional gal in a lot of ways." Then she stopped at the kitchen island and turned to face me, resting her plate on the granite.

With a smile and a wink, she added, "But I'm loosening up."

You were introduced to Josh at the book's beginning. Josh, to recall, is a dairy farmer in Massachusetts. He raises Brown Swiss, cows that are widely praised for their milk's fat-to-protein ratio, which makes it ideal for cheese making. And he belongs to a unique cooperative in which members share land, animals, equipment, and buildings. Upon buying into the cooperative, Josh joined three other households and had immediate access to infrastructure, land, and animals—specifically a small greenhouse, certified organic fields, two machine sheds, a barn and dairy parlor, and a herd of Brown Swiss.

I am returning to my visit with Josh thanks to a conversation we'd had about the "culture shock" he experienced when first exposed to a world where "sharing took precedence over individual property."

Culture shock?

The individual ownership economy's reach is deep, shaping not only what we do but also how we think and feel. This influence is not always apparent. Often it reveals itself only when one is confronted with a situation that doesn't conform to preconceived norms and expectations—culture shock.

The shock comes from having our individualism challenged. We value independence, for good reason. This, however, should not be confused with giving selfishness the green light. You can be independent without being a prick. We need to ask what we're producing with the status quo. Kids as young as three, after handling coins for a short period of time, have been shown repeatedly through experimental design to be less helpful and generous to their peers when compared with others who handled things such as similar-sized buttons and candy.[6]

Part of the reason, then, why many do not give a shit about sharing, to go back to Adam Berk's colorful quote at the chapter's beginning, is that we are socialized not to. Should we really be surprised to learn, then, that people are uncomfortable when placed in situations lubricated as much by trust and social capital as by money and contracts?

As my interview with Josh neared its end, we found refuge from the hot sun on the front porch of his decorative Victorian Painted Lady. I remember being frustrated, ironically, by a light breeze. Doing more harm than good, it circulated out the cool, shadowed relief with air that felt as if it had been blown from a hair dryer. The only consolation was that it was scented by the sweet smell of the wisteria vines and their blossoms overtaking the lattice next to the house. With me sitting on an

Adirondack chair and Josh on a swing, he told me about what he called "the transition"—a yearlong period that began just prior to his family's move to the cooperative.

Josh and his wife, Rosemary, had belonged to the cooperative for about five years. When they joined, their youngest child was fourteen and their oldest sixteen. He recalled what it was like to move into this new world and come to terms with it.

"In some ways, the kids had the hardest and easiest time adjusting." Leaning forward, Josh reached into his back pocket, pulled out his wallet, and showed me a family picture. It had been taken on the steps of the porch we were sitting on. His children are now both grown up, one in college, the other enlisted in the army, and their photos act as proxies for the real thing. With his eyes fixed on the picture, Josh added, "They were just dumbfounded by the idea." The *idea* being that their mom and dad *co*-owned their farm with three other families. "And that meant they shared things too"—a nod of the head in the direction of the boys' picture at the mention of *they*.

He recounted, for example, how his sons had loved raiding the family garden pre-transition. "They'd come home from school and spend hours playing with their toy tractors in the dirt and eating whatever was ready to be eaten," he explained with a smile and with pride in his voice, adding, "When we moved, they had to learn that the garden wasn't all theirs." The biggest challenge, however, was learning to share the strawberry bed. Previously they'd had to share only with the birds, an act made less painful thanks to netting. "To share with the other families, that almost killed them that first year."

It took that first year for his sons to get used to their new reality. But Josh assured me that they eventually "came around to things."

Josh admitted to going through a transition period too, along with his wife, which speaks to the extent that sole ownership is normalized in our culture. Here were two adults who had actively sought out a new way of life. Before the day of legally becoming co-owners, they had invested dozens of hours with an attorney, committed to a six-figure investment (co-owning a farm isn't free, or even cheap), and participated in countless get-togethers with their then prospective partners. *Intellectually*, they were both 100 percent behind the idea. Josh mentioned how they "both *knew*" they wanted to do something like this. It was something they had known for a really long time. And yet, these thoughts of co-ownership were initially not strong enough to override the unspoken socialization most of us receive over the course of living "normal" lives in an ownership economy.

Josh explained it this way: "I'll admit this now, that at first I think we liked the *idea* of cooperative ownership more than the actual practice. But we got used to it, with the help of the other community members"—that was another interesting point, that he referred to his co-owners as *community members*.

Five years in, where are Josh and his wife at now? With the "resocialization process complete"—Josh's term, though I could not have put it better myself—it sounded as if they would not want to live any other way.

Here's to establishing sharing habits early. Recognizing too that what is first uncomfortable can be made more manageable, normal even, when confronted together. We should not expect all types of sharing to work overnight.

So: if at first we don't succeed . . .

CHAPTER 8

From Pricks to Partners

I could smell my final destination before seeing it. Cookies? Cake? Nope, bread—freshly baked!

Bookended by a used clothing store and a pizzeria on a semi-busy boulevard in West Seattle, Washington, Bread and Stuff had been open for a little over a year when I met with Dorothy, the business owner, manager, chef, and baker.[1] When asked to describe her establishment in one sentence, she responded, pausing only long enough to swallow her sip of coffee, "Neighborhood café-bakery committed to the principle of sourcing from local organic farms."

It almost never was.

Sitting there with Dorothy, at one of those cool vintage laminate tables trimmed with metal, you would have never guessed she'd been homeless seven years before. That is right, living in shelters and, for a couple weeks, living in her car. *Homeless.*

"D-I-V-O-R-C-E. It wiped me out." Dorothy's ex had lacked self-control in ways I can and cannot write about. In terms of the former, he managed to charge his way to a $40,000 credit card debt. Dorothy learned about his shopping proclivities—he had a particular penchant for guns—only after the damage had been done. A knock on the door from a repo man is a heck of a way to learn about your loved one's problem and the fact that you're penniless.

By her own admission, Dorothy was "poor, straight-up broke." Even after finding her financial feet, at least enough to get out of her car and into a condo, which she still rents, Dorothy lacked perhaps the most important thing of all for any aspiring entrepreneur: C-R-E-D-I-T.

Even a perfect credit score would not have helped. She told of her sister, who at the time lived in another state, traveling to Seattle so they could both talk about her restaurant idea with a lending agent. "We were told that the bank was generally interested only in loans north of $60,000 or $70,000," she said. The bank did have an option for her and her sister: a credit card with, in Dorothy's words, "a crazy interest rate."

Dorothy had long dreamed of opening a restaurant. After her stint living out of a suitcase, she returned to cooking for family and friends, which she had started doing in high school. (She'd been too embarrassed to tell these friends she was homeless, in case you're wondering why they did not take her in during that difficult stretch.) "The idea was always there," she told me. "There was a lot of support; everyone told me how much they enjoyed my food. 'You should start a restaurant.' I heard that a lot."

Two friends and the sister helped bankroll her dream. She started small, making breads at home and selling them at local farmers' markets. After a year of building her brand, she had developed a devoted customer base—whenever she arrived at the market, she was greeted by a line of people waiting for her. The time seemed right to take the next step. Hopeful, she set off to find space and open Bread and Stuff.

This is where the lending agent came in—and where the story takes an exceptional turn, which, one hopes, will one day become unexceptional. If this were a typical small-business story, Dorothy would have either taken out a high interest loan, an incredibly risky venture, to say the least, or given up on Bread and Stuff. What happened instead is that one of her bread loving customers connected her with someone from Community Sourced Capital, a Seattle-based company whose online crowdfunding platform enables interest free loans.

CSC first started making loans in 2013. It is similar in many ways to the more familiar Kickstarter and GoFundMe, with one important innovation. CSC focuses specifically on raising funds within the community where the business will be located, from people committed to supporting local entrepreneurs.

Businesses approved for the platform run a four-week campaign. Before it begins, CSC charges a onetime $250 launch fee to build a campaign page telling potential investors a compelling story. Projects range from $5,000 to $50,000. Interested individuals can then buy "squares," each representing a $50 zero interest loan to the business. If the campaign is successful and all the money requested is earned, the business starts paying "squareholders" back immediately. Borrowers are typically allotted up to three years to make good on their loan. So far, 98 percent of CSC's loans either have been repaid or are in good standing.

"I couldn't believe my luck," Dorothy confessed, giving me a huge grin. She went on to describe the nature of the loan, and the savings it resulted in, as compared with what would have happened had she gone the high interest route suggested by her personal banker. Her CSC monthly payment was less than what her interest only payment would have been. No wonder she was smiling. I was too by the end of our conversation.

One burden associated with ownership is debt. To expect that we can rid the world of debt is about like asking that we rid it of conflict: you can ask, but don't hold your breath. Small steps. The amount of debt we choose to strap small businesses with is something we can and should control.

The Dorothys of the world want single-digit interest rates. Who doesn't? Financial institutions don't, for one. Wall Street has become quite content with double-digit—*triple*-digit, even—interest rates. Yet most bankers, and certainly those setting lending policy at the national level, do not call neighborhoods like the one where Bread and Stuff is located home.

If they did, things might be different.

Participants in peer-to-peer lending platforms generally understand that runaway interest rates are not only bad for these small businesses; they are also bad for communities. When you cannot pay off your principle because of interest rates, you do not have the time or resources to innovate, socially or otherwise, because all your energy is focused on generating revenue. How can we expect businesses to act responsibly, and do things like pay their workers a livable wage, if they are servicing their loan instead of their community? We cannot.

Dorothy put this point succinctly: "Those smaller monthly payments made all the difference for me, allowing me to reinvest in my community, making sure I do right to the people here. If I had gotten a loan through the bank, all my energy would have been in trying to make my mortgage. That's no way to serve a community."

And yet, national lending practices are heading in precisely the wrong direction.

The total volume of loans held by community banks peaked in 2008, only to drop rapidly with the Great Recession, bottoming out in 2011.[2] To make sense of this, I reached out to Stephan, who had worked until recently for the Federal Reserve System as a research officer. We talked about how banks, in the period leading up to the crisis, had relaxed underwriting standards and accepted applicants who had little equity, or even no equity in many cases, but who had wildly optimistic property appraisals and income forecasts. "After the crisis, that all stopped," Stephan explained. "It's a totally different ball game today, especially if you're looking for small-business financing. Most lenders, post-2008, are no longer community focused but are now Fed focused."

That last comment about banks being "Fed focused" was a reference to regulators' push to require banks to hold more capital against business loans than consumer loans, which has driven up the costs of small-business lending. "Small businesses are small because they don't have the credit of a Sam Walton," Stephan reminded me. Sam Walton, for those who do not recognize the name, founded Walmart and oversaw its expansion until his death in 1992.

The financial experts I talked with all mentioned how crises hit small businesses harder than they hit large firms, as small businesses are more dependent on bank capital to fund improvements, repairs, and lulls in revenue. Job data from the recession support this assertion. From the employment peak prior to the financial crisis until the numbers bottomed out, in March 2009, small firms shed 11 percent of their jobs. Among businesses with fewer than fifty employees, the decline was even greater: 14.1 percent. Payrolls at larger businesses declined by roughly 7 percent during the same period.[3]

These numbers are especially hard to stomach when you consider the importance of small businesses to regional economies and household well-being. Since 1995, small businesses have been responsible for creating approximately two of every three new jobs. Half of the 28 million small firms in the United States are home based, and 23 million are sole proprietorships. The remaining 5 million have employees and can be divided into mom-and-pop enterprises, small and medium sized suppliers, and high growth start-ups.

Each of these small businesses creates a multiplier effect or dollar turnover—the number of times a given dollar results in other local transactions. Locally owned companies tend to buy locally when it comes to the services of attorneys, accountants, graphic designers, carpet cleaners, window washers, and so on. In contrast, large chains handle many of these services internally—at "corporate"—to capture economies of scale. These corporate savings, however, come at the expense of local economies.

Among the thousands of small-scale food entrepreneurs with whom I have interacted over the years, I cannot think of one company that did not rely heavily on its local economy for its supplies and services. Like most of us—my household included—they used Amazon and other "distant" suppliers. But when it came to doing taxes, painting walls, and repairing equipment, they looked locally. That is not the same story I hear from most of the CEOs and managers of large national chains whom I know. As reliant as Main Street is on, well, Main Street, national chains find it more efficient to obtain services and products from other large national, sometimes transnational, firms.

A study from the Maine Center for Economic Policy calculated that every $100 spent at locally owned businesses within the state generated an additional $58 thanks to those store owners having turned their dollars over within the community. For comparison, $100 spent at national chains generated only $33 in local impact, mostly through employee wages and rents. Small businesses, in other words, were found to generate a 76 percent greater return to the local economy than when money was spent at big-box outlets.[4]

These findings mirror research that focused on Salt Lake City, Utah. In one study, locally owned retail establishments and restaurants returned 52 percent and 78.6 percent, respectively, of their revenue to the surrounding economy. By comparison, the national retail chains examined—Barnes & Noble, Home Depot, Office Max, and Target— recirculated an average of 13.6 percent of their revenue. The three restaurant chains examined—Darden, McDonald's, and P.F. Chang's— returned an average of 30.4 percent of revenue to the surrounding economy.[5]

And that is just their economic benefits. The social value of these enterprises, while perhaps harder to quantify, are no less significant.

David Brown at the University of Colorado has described how the presence of Walmart—arguably the antithesis of Main Street retail—in a community is correlated, at statistically significant levels, with *decreases* in voter turnout and participation in political activities, *lower* levels of philanthropy, and *declines* in social capital. This pattern was observed in four different data sets based on data at county and individual levels.[6] "The results," he wrote, "imply Wal-Mart has a measurable impact on communities in the United States that reaches beyond prices, income, and employment. Big box retail, it seems, comes at a cost. Lower prices and all that comes with them hold important consequences for political participation."[7]

These findings parallel those reported in an article in the *American Journal of Agricultural Economics,* not an outlet known for its boat rocking publications. Authors Stephan Goetz and Anil Rupasingha concluded that the presence of a Walmart in a county is correlated with lower levels of social capital—fewer social networks and less trust, for example.[8]

Correlation, I know, is not causation. We need to ask why: *why* might the presence of national chains, such as Walmart, cost us as citizens? I can offer a couple of general observations in response to this question. First, national chains tend to foster *car*-munities, as they are often confined to a community's outskirts—the only place that could accommodate their massive footprint and parking lot.[9] Their car-centric business model becomes a type of self-fulfilling prophecy. This happens when locally owned mom-and-pop options, sited, literally, on Main Street and thus more easily accessed by bike and on foot, are shuttered thanks to Fed focused lending policies. The walkability of a community is one of the strongest predictors of it having high social capital levels.[10]

My second observation simply picks up where the first leaves off: as national chains extract more wealth than they generate and leave in these spaces, communities suffer *as communities*. Financial inequalities exacerbate social distance, resulting in people who feel they have less in common with their neighbors.[11]

It is a lot easier to do the right thing as a business when shareholders, community members, and customers are one and the same. It is a different beast entirely when the person signing your paycheck—or loan—does not give a crap about whether Main Street is littered with potholes or the high school's ceiling leaks every time it rains.

To quote Craig, a Seattleite and owner of a small ice cream parlor who also happened to get his business off the ground with a peer-to-peer loan, "Small business owners generally follow the credo 'You don't shit where you eat.'"

His point, restated in child appropriate language: small businesses succeed by taking care of their communities, not by exploiting them.

Craig's crass credo came to mind about a week later, while I was talking with Marcela.

In her mid-fifties, Marcela had auburn hair, large dark eyes, and fine high cheekbones that gave her solidly sculpted face a look of authority. And then she spoke. I doubt I am the first person to do a double take upon first hearing her high pitched voice.

I was drawn to Marcela because she was both a peer-to-peer borrower and a peer-to-peer lender. In the world of Fed focused lending, this dual identity would be considered positively schizophrenic. Conventional banks do not borrow from their borrowers.

Turns out there are a lot of people out there like Marcela. These individuals started at the receiving end of a community loan, enjoyed the experience, and decided to pay it forward by funding a peer-to-peer loan to help some aspiring entrepreneur.

Marcela lives in North Carolina and is the owner-operator of a bakery that specializes in eastern European pastries. At one point in our conversation, she shared with me how lenders and borrowers were matched up through the platform Slow Money NC. Loans can be made only between people in the same community, which I later learned includes people in the same or even adjacent counties. The purpose of this, Marcela told me, is so "borrower and lender, or lenders, as there's usually more than one, stay connected."

Not all peer-to-peer loans are interest free. Those made through Slow Food NC are interest bearing, though the rate is many points below that of a conventional small-business loan. I mention this to highlight that social dividends are not the only returns being sought through these arrangements.

While community based loans are far less restrictive than Fed focused loans, and therefore more "risky" in the eyes of conventional loan officers, their default rates remain remarkably low: between 1 percent and 4 percent among the lending platforms that I examined. Compare this with the failure rate of conventional small-business loans made prior to the financial crisis, back when banks were looser with their underwriting requirements: 12 percent.[12]

There's a very simple reason why peer-to-peer loans have lower default rates: borrower and lender are socially connected. It is a lot harder to willfully default on a loan when it comes from a friend, which is precisely what lenders become in a lot of these instances. Meanwhile, at the other end of the loan, lenders do not want to see their friends (and investments) fail, so most do what they can to support them.

We are taught that the economy principally generates wealth. If those transactions happen to create social benefits, great, but the ultimate source of well-being is money. According to this outlook, social gains are usually incurred indirectly, *through* wealth. Peer-to-peer lending tells a different story, in which economic benefits occur *because of* social dividends—money isn't the driver; it's just a nice side effect.

It is a case of what's old is new again, lest we forget that the word "economics" is derived from the ancient Greek word for management of the household: *oikonomika*. According to Aristotle, the economy is composed of two interrelated systems. One speaks to phenomena such as money and market transactions, what we tend to think of when calling the term to mind. Yet without the other component, the whole financial house of cards comes tumbling down. Think of all those non-market exchange relationships that make life not only worth living but also *livable*.

The futurist Alvin Toffler famously asked a room full of CEOs what it would cost their respective firms if all new employees had not been toilet trained and they had to pay for this preparation. Toffler's point is much the same as Aristotle's: markets would not exist without nonmarket actions. The world would be a shitty place were it not for all those nonmonetized activities.

Take Marcela's experience with her peer lender, who had received a fairly sizable inheritance after her mother passed away. The lender, in Marcela's words, wanted "to do something that gave back to her community while also generating some modest financial return."

Marcela swiveled her chair, reached for a framed photo resting on a bookshelf, and handed it to me. I immediately recognized the face—those well defined cheekbones were a dead giveaway. I was looking at a picture of a very happy Marcela. She had one arm around someone I did not recognize. Both were giving the familiar thumbs-up sign. "That's me and Josée," the lender, "the day I got my loan." That explained Marcela's ear-to-ear smile.

Looking back, I realized that the very fact that she had that picture spoke volumes about the relationship. I mentioned this once to a loan officer at a conventional bank, asking if his picture adorns the offices of many small-business owners. He answered immediately, with a deep, chesty laugh: "Oh sure, I make lots of friends doing this; that's why I never see any of them again."

Back to Marcela: "Josée was always promoting my business among friends, on Facebook, at her work." Marcela also admitted that knowing her lender "created extra incentive to not let her down." I don't think I've ever met a small-business owner who was concerned about defaulting for the sake of a Fed focused lender.

Marcela's sentiments square with findings from the vast literature on microlending programs.[13] This form of financing is usually put to work in low-income countries, where small amounts of money are loaned to poor entrepreneurs to encourage self-sufficiency and to alleviate economic hardship. These programs also focus on providing *social* support, mentoring, training, and the like.

"It's a virtuous cycle." Clearly excited, Marcela began to wave her arms in a motion that looked like a mix between practicing karate and conducting a band. Her voice took on an aggressive quality that masked the childlike qualities I had come to expect.

"Peer-to-peer lending creates an entirely new business model, from survival-of-the-fittest to we're-all-in-this-together."

Oikonomika.

Have you ever met someone who was sweet and kind and funny and had almost nothing in common with you? I'd place Arlene in that box—constantly asking if I would like anything to eat or drink, making dopey jokes that were often self-deprecating, and regularly using profanity to punctuate points. She also had an infectious "playground" laugh. Where we differed, and significantly, were in our respective pedigrees. She was the child of a once famous Hollywood actress, had dated a duke, and had once made out with an Oscar winner.

I met with Arlene at her house in California's Central Valley. A three-time lender of zero interest peer-to-peer loans at the time of our interview, Arlene had been in finance before retiring. She admitted to wishing she had taken a different, albeit related, career path. "If crowd-funding would have been a thing twenty years ago, I would have gladly shifted jobs."

Not long into the conversation, Arlene dropped the following comment: "Money doesn't have to make you a prick." Initially, I was not sure whether she was defending her well-to-do upbringing or commenting about something else. Turns out she was making a positive point about peer-to-peer lending.

Her point is well taken; money is correlated with unsociable outcomes. This is not a social commentary about people who have a lot of money. The mere presence of money, even the *thought* of it in some instances, can make you, well, a prick.

The first research I am aware of on this subject dates back to 2006, when Kathleen Vohs, at the University of Minnesota's Carlson School of Management, and her colleagues published an article titled "The Psychological Consequences of Money" in the journal *Science*.[14] In one study, participants were primed by the presence of a large pile of Monopoly money. Those exposed to the play money were less willing to help someone who "accidentally" spilled a box of pencils. In another scenario, participants were asked to fill out questionnaires while seated in front of a computer monitor with a screen saver that depicted either money floating or fish swimming. Exposure to the floating cash reduced participants' willingness to work in a team and resulted in their seeing themselves as having less in common with the other participants. Vohs and her collaborators even tried having their subjects unscramble phrases that included words such as "salary" while a control group worked with nonmonetary terms. These seemingly mundane tasks reproduced similar outcomes. The nonmoney group spent an average of three minutes on a difficult puzzle before reaching out for help, while members of the money group plodded away for more than five minutes. Those who unscrambled nonmonetary phrases also spent, on average, roughly twice as much time helping a struggling peer with the puzzle than did those who had been primed to think about money. These findings have since been replicated through a number of other experimental designs.[15]

Arlene pretty much nailed it with the "prick" comment.

Unfortunately, the research does not consider whether people using sharing platforms respond differently when in the presence of money. Arlene would argue that they would act differently, or at least could; after all, not all sharing platforms are the same. I would tend to agree. I have talked with enough people experimenting with sharing to say some of these practices most definitely have that potential.

Arlene again: "It isn't money per se that's alienating but how it tends to be exchanged in today's economy. Money has become a proxy, a substitute, for social relationships, whereas with peer-to-peer lending it is a vehicle that amplifies community engagement." Arlene was speaking to points made earlier about the creation of an economy that takes care of its *entire* household—*oikonomika*. This stands in contrast to conventional markets, which turn you into . . . well, you know.

Arlene spent a lot of time talking about her experiences with peer-to-peer lending and why she would have "gladly" left her job as a financial planner for a career in crowdfunding small businesses. She also told me stories from her financial planning days—four, actually. While the characters differed, the story arc was always the same. An individual with high minded aspirations visits her office to plan for his or her retirement and expresses clear wishes about which sectors to avoid investing in. She mentioned one guy, for instance, who was "initially gung-ho about social justice" and gave her clear directions to avoid making investments in Big Food and Big Pharma companies. But after a year or two, the clients all started leaving those convictions at the door. "It doesn't take long for someone to look at their statements and start seeing *only* money. Injustices aren't exactly spelled out in annual investment reports." Sounding incredulous, Arlene added, "I was helping people sell out."

With that, she looked me squarely in the eyes. Shrugging her shoulders as if to say "I told you so," she continued, "That's what happens when people get close to money and not to the people behind it."

This does not happen as easily when money is rooted in one's community.

A few minutes later in the conversation, Arlene got up, walked over to a nearby closet, and disappeared for a few seconds. Emerging holding a purse, she returned to her seat and set it on her lap. Releasing the two clasps—*click-click*—she opened it and pulled out a bright red wallet from which she produced three pictures. *No way*, I remember thinking. Setting them down on the table between us, she pointed to one with a woman standing behind one of those old-timey cash registers. Pushing the photo toward me with her index finger, she added, "Lending that comes from a community never stops being part of that community, you see?"

I am not sure I really did see at the time. But I think I do now. Lenders rallying their Facebook friends to eat at the establishment their loan is helping to support; lenders and borrowers with pictures on their desks or in their wallets of peers at the other "end" of the exchange, all smiles, positioned next to school photos of their kids; people with annual incomes well south of the nation's average (the average income in the United States in 2016 was $50,756) participating in these arrangements; businesses in search of social dividends and not just financial rewards: that's community lending.

Lending that comes from a community never stops being part of that community, you see? I do now, Arlene.

CHAPTER 9
Food Sovereignty

Runaway inequality is placing tremendous pressure on the world's democracies and on our international capacity for peace. The widespread loss of security among the world's middle and working classes has produced a Janus-faced response: one listening to our better angels and seeking equity, the other preying on our fears, looking to blame anyone with, say, brown or black skin. "They're stealing our jobs!" Spoken just like someone who has never met, let alone worked or eaten alongside or shared with, an immigrant laborer. Meanwhile, our social, political, and economic institutions are teetering on the brink of collapse—climate change, racist candidates being elected to positions of great political power, unparalleled concentrations of wealth and property, and on and on.

One of our major tasks ahead therefore involves rebuilding a food economy that is sufficiently participatory. We need something that allows our household (*oikonomika*) to flourish while reinvigorating our sense of democracy.

I am hopeful, in part because I believe in letting hopes rather than hurts shape our future. But also because I have witnessed what can be accomplished, what *has been* accomplished, when people work together and share. This is where the concept of sovereignty comes into the picture, the idea that independence, freedom, and choice arise out of interdependence. The at-each-other's-throats type of individualism privileged in some corners of our economy is not only wrong; it's dangerous.

At the book's beginning, I touched on the meaning of food sovereignty. The concept speaks to the sweet spot where *access*, *knowledge* exchange, and *community* building overlap. Seed saving and sharing, cooperative arrangements that help farmers negotiate fair prices, cooking classes that empower individuals and communities: those are all terribly important activities. Yet sovereignty cannot be reduced to a single set of practices. Instead, the ultimate power of food sovereignty lies in its ability to help practitioners live an alternative way of life because it gives those practicing it a different view of life.

The book *Keywords*, written by the iconoclastic, tweed-wearing Welsh academic and literary critic Raymond Williams, offers a unique perspective on worldviews.[1] As eyes are to the soul, according to Williams, words are portals into the assumptions that animate our world. This makes inquiry into our shared vocabulary of immense practical consequence. Put simply, it is not enough to say "We ought to share" without also understanding the worldviews that guide and inform that declarative statement.

I recently witnessed the interaction between words, practices, and worldviews on a trip to California. I cannot say exactly where I was or name the two groups I was studying because of the politically sensitive nature of our discussions. People avoid talking on the record if perceived costs outweigh perceived benefits—I'll be honest, there are few of the latter that come with talking to me if you inhabit a world that privileges individualism and short-term gain. To encourage participation, I therefore promised to keep the city as well as the organizations involved anonymous.

I can say that one group was an urban farming cooperative; the other, a commission that informed food and agricultural policy in the state and was aligned with industry. Thirty-eight from the urban cooperative were interviewed and another thirty-five from the industry based commission. The cooperative sample was diverse, especially compared with the relatively homogeneous (read mostly white, mostly male, all affluent) industry group. Annual household incomes ranged from below $15,000 to two reporting in the $100,000 to $124,999 category. The cooperative members described their ethnicities as 11 Asian Americans, 11 African Americans, 9 Mexican Americans/Latinos, 6 whites, and 1 Native American. Twenty were women and eighteen were men.

The land in the cooperative was in a community trust. Members produced food for personal household use, but they also pooled their harvest and sold to local restaurants and other members of the community. In addition to producing food, they held workshops on things such as seed saving, compost making, and cooking. They also made raised beds for gardening for members of the community to promote urban agriculture, healthy eating, and food access. These beds were sold at market rate to those who could afford them, allowing the cooperative to offer subsidized rates to those who couldn't; in some cases they even gave the beds away. As for the soil used to fill the new beds: it came from compost generated in-house, made from garden waste as well as from food waste from surrounding restaurants that purchased from the cooperative.

One day sticks in my mind. I spent the morning talking with individuals associated with California's food and agriculture industry as they attended a "summit" at a swanky hotel; in the afternoon, I walked across the street to meet with some cooperative members at a café. Later that evening, processing the events of the day, I went to one of those twenty-four-hour greasy spoons where people in the movies go when they cannot sleep. I was shocked by just how different responses were between the groups.

In order to gauge their ideas about sovereignty, I had asked individuals to select three terms that they associated with, respectively, "social justice" and "autonomy." Prior to answering, they were shown a list of roughly fifty terms for each keyword—words that I thought they might choose, on the basis of my decades of experience in talking with groups like this. The terms on this list were defined to ensure that all participants were operating from a shared understanding of concepts. I then used software to generate "word clouds"—graphics that show the most often used terms in large letters, the least often used terms in smaller letters—based on their responses. Words mentioned fewer than three times were not included, to improve the figures' readability.

Want to see what sovereignty looks like? Have a look at the worldview that animated the industry group's way of life, and compare that with the one expressed by the cooperative members.

I appreciate word clouds because they can help us visualize data, and they offer more immediately stark images than any text could. Yet, in the end, there is no substitute for text. Data do not speak for themselves, as I tell my students. So it is at this point where I roll up my sleeves and do my best to be a ventriloquist.

The daylight dimmed to gold. Crickets had begun their song: a musical *knee-knee* that I imagined as the first movement of a suite soon

Figure 9.1

Figure 9.2

Sovereignty Community
Liberty
Independence Relationships
Authority Self-reliance
Liberty States rights
Individualism
Free will
Self-determination
Control Freedom
Survival of the fittest
Self rule

FIGURE 9.3

Mutual support
Reciprocity
Collaboration
Independence
Companionship Democracy
Friendship Individualism
Interdependence
Solidarity Freedom
Relationships
Cooperation
Teamwork
Community

FIGURE 9.4

to build and include the bass line of frogs and the pyrotechnics of lightning bugs. Michael and I were seated on a stone bench, which, still warm from the midday sun, heated our lower halves while the cooling air of the approaching evening chilled our tops. The bench rested next to the herbs in his shared garden plot.

Michael was a middle-aged African American and a longtime co-operative member. He had one of those voices that sounded as though it were coming directly from his chest and that consequently made yours sound as if you were talking through a bamboo tube.

As we reflected on the urban agriculture cooperative, the conversation moved to the topic of social justice: (Figure 9.1 and 9.2 offer "social justice" word clouds for industry and cooperative examples, respectively. Figures 9.3 and 9.4 offer "autonomy" word clouds for industry and cooperative samples, respectively.) I had not completed the word cloud exercise by this point, though I was aware that the two groups had very different views about this keyword.

When describing the concept, Michael wanted to be sure that I understood how its focus ought to be less on "the rights that people have and more about what people are *actually able to do.*" Those final few words came out like a rattling thunderbolt that I could feel in my own chest. This view stands in contrast to how those from the industry sample tended to talk about social justice. For them, the concept centered on the idea of rights, of making sure people have equal treatment in the eyes of the law and the market (note the terms "fair laws" and "free market" in their word clouds), irrespective of outcomes.

Not that the former outlook is unique. Prior chapters are filled with people who understand that social justice hinges on access and capabilities as much as on rights. People have the right to shop, buy, and eat whatever they want. But that doesn't mean they have the ability to do so. Yes, adults can legally go to any store they wish, and have the right to buy anything there in exchange for money, just as anyone can legally own land and farm or start a restaurant. But we all know those rights are not always realized. This in itself is not problematic. I know people who think they would love to farm but who, if I am honest, shouldn't—no business acumen, no green thumb, and, perhaps most problematic of all for one or two of them, they routinely sleep in past noon.

My concern is for those with the skills, passions, and sleep habits that suggest they could succeed if given the opportunity. They are not given a fair shake largely because they lack capital and credit. The previous chapters offer rich examples in which, through collaboration and sharing, people are able to realize those rights, together.

Perhaps the most memorable thing about my time with cooperative members was that no one seemed ever—*ever*—to have worked alone. (I am all too aware of many farmers' relatively lonely existence. Having myself sat in tractor and combine cabs for hours on end during harvest and planting season, I know this isolation firsthand. And while farmers certainly work with others, the level of collaboration witnessed never approached what I observed at this urban agriculture cooperative or at, to take an example from prior chapters, Josh's farming community.) Turning compost, caging tomatoes, constructing raised beds, planting, weeding, harvesting, fixing communally owned shovels and pitchforks, sharpening hoes, delivering produce to restaurants, picking up food waste from restaurants: being a cooperative member meant being continually with others. And, most striking of all, these interactions involved *diverse* others—white, black, Christian, Muslim, Democrat, Socialist, Republican, Asian, gay, lesbian. . . .[2]

To say it was coincidence that terms such as "collaboration," "cooperation," "interdependence," and "solidarity" appeared regularly in the "autonomy" word cloud for this population is to be blind to the power of practice, habit, and socialization. And the fact that the industry group offered no mention of these terms when defining "autonomy," instead painting a polar opposite worldview with such terms as "individualism," "self-reliance," "self-determination," and "survival of the fittest," only strengthens my conviction that this observation is significant. The industry group's "autonomy" word cloud is actually a textbook representation of what scholars call the "ideology of individualism," the life giving atmosphere in which at-your-throat capitalism thrives.[3] It reflects an understanding of autonomy that leads individuals to see neighbors as natural competitors—no wonder so many think good fences make good neighbors.

It was late in the afternoon when I arrived at the cooperative's gardens on my final day. I would be flying back to Colorado the next morning. A handful of tall shadows stretched across a flower bed: men and women standing, talking together. Noticing me, a woman broke away and walked in my direction. She lifted both arms over her head, like a boxer being announced as winner in the center of the ring. I had an appointment with Colleen.

We decided to take a walk as we talked. We headed west, facing the setting sun, its power decreased considerably. Like an invisible hand perched above the horizon, Earth's atmosphere had started to elongate the sun's shape and weaken its rays.

Colleen recalled her "initiation into a cooperative way of life." She was relatively new to the area and thus to the community. She had been a member for roughly four months. She admitted to initially having been uncomfortable with the way some things were done. "It was an adjustment getting used to how decisions are not executively made but come about through consensus, dialogue, and, if necessary, a little horse-trading."

Yet with practice—literally, *doing* sharing and collaboration—this apprehension receded. Colleen again: "After an initial transition period, I became acclimated to my new world"—interesting choice of words, *new world*—"to the point that I now find myself wanting to collaborate even outside the cooperative."

To show that this change had produced for her not only a new way of life but also a new *view* of life, she proceeded to tell me a story about an instance at her job in which her manager had made a decision without input and how that had greatly upset her. "That reaction wouldn't have happened before my joining the co-op," she told me. She then turned her head and lifted her right hand, shielding her eyes from the sun. The effect, though casting much of her face in shadow, made her eyes sparkle against the darkness. She was intently looking at me, unblinkingly, seriously. "It changed me, I just hope for the best."

I think you can rest assured that it has.

The Union Kitchen was a hive of activity—abuzz with movement and accentuated with an incredible mix of smells and sounds. Those participating shared space in a fully equipped commercial kitchen, where they could rent anything they needed to make their food.

I have already discussed what a challenge it can be to start a food business. In Washington, DC, the only thing harder to do than throw a rock in any direction and not hit a lawyer is to find affordable commercial real estate. So, in late 2012, restaurateurs Jonas Singer and Cullen Gilchrist opened Union Kitchen in a 680-square-meter warehouse.

Cornelia and I were connected through a mutual friend. Her specialty was corned beef, which she made for area restaurants. She rented from Union Kitchen a couple of tables, cooktop use, and some storage space in a refrigerator.

While cleaning up her prep area, having just placed her beef in a giant tub for a seven-day soak (the essential brining process), she talked about how the sharing economy might assuage the worst of the world's demons while strengthening its angels. Putting lids back on spice containers, she confessed to "wondering whether the present food economy is sustainable," adding, "The sun might be setting on how we've conventionally thought about things."

Sadly, outside of sharing circles especially, it seems people have an easier time imagining the end of civilization than anything beyond the conventional ownership economy. I was not sure whether Cornelia would add a rejoinder about how we are going to fix things. Often there isn't one.

Drawing a line through spilled ground cinnamon at her work space, Cornelia had a think. "Conventional economies can never be free or freeing, thanks to market concentration," she explained as she wiped her fingers on her apron. "We've got to move away from systems that perpetuate hierarchies and positional power."

Hierarchies? Positional power? Rather than invite clarification, I decided to let silence ask the question for me. After a few seconds of direct eye contact and the best inquisitive look I could purposefully muster, she filled the void.

"The thing that draws a lot of people into these new engagements is the possibility to challenge structures, to empower people rather than corporations."

With this comment, I felt a faint pulse: something away on the horizon, tugging, something I had felt before. Cornelia's assertion about what animates participation in these sharing engagements is apropos for a concluding chapter. Her solo is actually a chorus. Of the more than two hundred people interviewed for this book, most had been drawn to these practices to shake things up.

That might be exactly what we need: for each of us to scream, *I'm as mad as hell, and I'm not going to take this anymore!* And maybe, just maybe, some of the practices described herein can be used to give this primal scream some direction, while inspiring others on the sideline to take action too.

"And for God's sake, we need to stop looking for 'the Uber of food.' Any model that concentrates wealth at the top isn't worth emulating. You can't put lipstick on a turd and think that will fix the stink"—as I've said, there is something pretty crappy about a business that sucks wealth from communities.

We've come full circle, as I criticized heavily the Uber platform in the introduction. A convenient ride and a means for middle-income households to supplement their income: beyond that, this popular sharing platform provides very little else. There certainly is nothing about Uber that would cause participants to rethink their keywords; nothing to suggest the experience affords people greater feelings of solidarity or empathy toward those different from themselves; nothing to make them feel like screaming about how mad they are at the current individual ownership economy.

That is where the real potential lies in many of the previously described spaces. Creating access to stuff, exchanging knowledge, and building communities are all important. Finding ways to encourage sharing platforms that serve multiple ends ought to be a priority, which in some cases starts by making sure the activities are legal. But remember also, as illustrated powerfully with the word clouds, the value of these spaces cannot be confined to their existence as exchange mediums.

To evoke the often misunderstood aphorism by Marshall McLuhan, the medium is the message.[4] This phrase actually means that the form of a medium, in this case *the experiences* afforded by certain sharing platforms, embeds itself in any message, such as how we *understand* certain keywords. Were it not for the word clouds, I would not dare speak in such grand tones. But you have seen the data, so I'll dare: some of these practices appear to be world creating. I do not know how else to describe it—one group, for example, equating "fair laws" and the "free market" to "social justice"; the other, describing the keyword with terms such as "equity" and "fair trade"—but to talk of different *worlds.* Colleen from the prior section, if you recall, used the same term when describing her transition to a life predicated on sharing and collaboration.

In those worlds, where collaboration supplants an at-each-other's-throats ethos, lie the seeds of something with the potential to decenter the individual ownership universe.

Here's to our Copernicus moment: to sharing that affords food sovereignty.

Notes

Introduction: Ownership through Sharing

1. Jim Blasingame, "Business Ownership Comes with Privileges," *Forbes*, April 1, 2013, www.forbes.com/sites/jimblasingame/2013/04/01/business-ownership-comes-with-privileges/#18da39bd6f43, accessed December 5, 2016.

2. Juli Obudzinski, "Beginning Farmer Policy Options for the Next Farm Bill," *Choices*, 4th quarter 2016, www.choicesmagazine.org/choices-magazine/theme-articles/theme-overview-addressing-the-challenges-of-entry-into-farming/beginning-farmer-policy-options-for-the-next-farm-bill.

3. Alicia Harvie, "A Looming Crisis on American Farms," Farm Aid, April 13, 2017, www.farmaid.org/blog/fact-sheet/looming-crisis-american-farms/.

4. Jarrett Bellini, "The No. 1 Thing to Consider before Opening a Restaurant," *CNBC*, March 15, 2016, www.cnbc.com/2016/01/20/heres-the-real-reason-why-most-restaurants-fail.html.

5. Adam Ozimek, "No, Most Restaurants Don't Fail in the First Year," *Forbes*, January 29, 2017, www.forbes.com/sites/modeledbehavior/2017/01/29/no-most-restaurants-dont-fail-in-the-first-year/#14d9b48d4fcc.

6. "The Rise of the Sharing Economy," *Economist*, March 9, 2013, www.economist.com/news/leaders/21573104-internet-everything-hire-rise-sharing-economy.

7. Food and Agriculture Organization of the United Nations, "Food Wastage Footprint: Impacts on Natural Resources; Summary Report," 2013, www.fao .org/docrep/018/i3347e/i3347e.pdf. See also, e.g., Anna Lee, "We're Throwing Away Tons of Fruits and Veggies for Not Being Pretty Enough," *Washington Post*, March 13, 2015, www.washingtonpost.com/opinions/eat-the -crooked-carrot-save-the-world/2015/03/13/d6899452-c7fb-11e4-a199 -6cb5e63819d2_story.html?utm_term=.249b006fe5e6.

8. See, e.g., Robert McHugh, "Aldi Ireland Donates 500,000 Meals to Charity through FoodCloud," *Business World*, November 14, 2016, www .businessworld.ie/agricultural-news/Aldi-Ireland-donates-500-000-meals -to-charity-through-FoodCloud-566538.html, accessed June 11, 2017.

9. "How Much Are People Making from the Sharing Economy?," *Earnest* (blog), June 13, 2017, www.earnest.com/blog/sharing-economy-income -data/.

10. Harry Campbell, "RSG 2017 Survey Results: Driver Earnings, Satisfaction, and Demographics," *The Rideshare Guy* (blog), January 17, 2017, https://the rideshareguy.com/rsg-2017-survey-results-driver-earnings-satisfaction-and -demographics/.

11. See, e.g., Joann Weiner, "The Hidden Costs of Being an Uber Driver," *Washington Post*, February 20, 2015, www.washingtonpost.com/news/get-there /wp/2015/02/20/the-hidden-costs-of-being-an-uber-driver/?utm_term =.5540ab991241.

12. See Alexandrea J. Ravenelle, "Sharing Economy Workers: Selling, Not Sharing," *Cambridge Journal of Regions, Economy and Society* 10, no. 2 (July 2017): 281–295, doi:10.1093/cjres/rsw043; Juliet B. Schor, "Does the Sharing Economy Increase Inequality within the Eighty Percent? Findings from a Qualitative Study of Platform Providers," *Cambridge Journal of Regions, Economy and Society* 10, no. 2 (July 2017): 263–279, doi:10.1093/cjres /rsw047.

13. David Kocieniewski, "The Sharing Economy Doesn't Share the Wealth," *Bloomberg Businessweek*, April 6, 2016, www.bloomberg.com/news/arti cles/2016-04-06/the-sharing-economy-doesn-t-share-the-wealth, accessed June 17, 2017.

14. Casey Newton, "This Is Uber's Playbook for Sabotaging Lyft," *Verge*, August 26, 2014, www.theverge.com/2014/8/26/6067663/this-is-ubers-play book-for-sabotaging-lyft.

15. Dara Kerr, "Uber Tests Taking 30% Commission from New Drivers," CNET, May 18, 2015, www.cnet.com/news/uber-tests-30-commission-for -new-drivers-in-san-francisco/, accessed January 18, 2018.

16. Paul Goddin, "Uber's Plan for Self-Driving Cars Bigger than Its Taxi Disruption," *Mobility Lab*, August 18, 2015, https://mobilitylab.org/2015 /08/18/ubers-plan-for-self-driving-cars-bigger-than-its-taxi-disruption/, accessed January 18, 2017.

17. See, e.g., Matt Ovenden, "Why the Peer-to-Peer Phenomenon Is the Next Big Thing," *Talk Business*, September 14, 2017, www.talk-business.co.uk /2017/09/14/why-the-peer-to-peer-phenomenon-is-the-next-big-thing/, accessed January 18, 2018.

18. Names of respondents have been changed to fulfill my promise of protecting their anonymity in exchange for being provided frank, honest responses.

19. While often attributed to the 1996 World Food Summit, the actual genealogy of the term is contested. See Marc Edelman, "Food Sovereignty: Forgotten Genealogies and Future Regulatory Challenges," *Journal of Peasant Studies* 41, no. 6 (January 2014): 959–978, doi:10.1080/03066150.2013. 876998.

20. Claire Provost, "La Via Campesina Celebrates 20 Years of Standing Up for Food Sovereignty," *Guardian* (US edition), June 17, 2013, www.the guardian.com/global-development/poverty-matters/2013/jun/17/la-via -campesina-food-sovereignty.

21. Michael Carolan, *The Real Cost of Cheap Food*, 2nd ed. (New York: Routledge, 2018).

22. See also Ashley M. Colpaart, "Exploring Personal, Business, and Community Barriers and Opportunities for Food Entrepreneurs" (PhD diss., Colorado State University, Fort Collins, 2017), https://search.proquest.com /openview/f6b0da9f807878951b7dc6b7b6cd8a59/1?pq-origsite=gscholar &cbl=18750&diss=y, accessed January 17, 2018.

23. This quote comes from Alexander den Heijer; see, e.g., www.alexander denheijer.com/single-post/2016/08/05/When-a-flower-doesnt-bloom.

Chapter 1: A Nightmare Realized

1. Jesse Newman, "U.S. Farm Income to Fall to Lowest Level in Nine Years," *Wall Street Journal*, August 25, 2015, www.wsj.com/articles/u-s-farm-income

-to-fall-to-lowest-level-in-nine-years-1440521337, accessed December 7, 2016; U.S. Department of Agriculture, "Highlights from the November 2016 Farm Income Forecast," 2016, www.ers.usda.gov/topics/farm-economy /farm-sector-income-finances/highlights-from-the-farm-income-forecast/, accessed December 7, 2016.

2. Minus food wholesaler numbers for New Zealand, as those data could not be obtained.

3. Kyle Wiens, "We Can't Let John Deere Destroy the Very Idea of Owner-ship," *Wired*, April 21, 2015, www.wired.com/2015/04/dmca-ownership -john-deere/, accessed December 14, 2016.

4. Thomas Fox-Brewster, "DMCA Ruling Ensures You Can't Be Sued for Hack-ing Your Car, Your Games, or Your iPhone," *Forbes*, October 27, 2015, www .forbes.com/sites/thomasbrewster/2015/10/27/right-to-tinker-victory /#58a0f4b838ae, accessed December 14, 2016.

5. John Deere Shared Services, Inc., "License Agreement for John Deere Em-bedded Software," www.deere.com/privacy_and_data/docs/agreement_pdfs /english/2016-10-28-Embedded-Software-EULA.pdf.

6. Sterling A. Bone, Glenn L. Christensen, and Jerome D. Williams, "Re-jected, Shackled, and Alone: The Impact of Systemic Restricted Choice on Minority Consumers' Construction of Self," *Journal of Consumer Research* 41, no. 2 (August 2014): 451–474, doi:10.1086/676689.

Chapter 2: When Sharing Is Illegal

1. In *Tony and Susan Alamo Foundation v. Secretary of Labor*, 471 U.S. 290, 302 (1985), the U.S. Supreme Court ruled that even those who "vehemently protest coverage under the Act" must be treated to the same legal tests as everyone else on the question of what labor projections apply to them.

2. See the U.S. Supreme Court case *Tennessee Coal Co. v. Muscoda Local No. 123*, 321 U.S. 590 (1944). The Court ruled as follows: "The Act [Fair Labor Standards Act] thus requires that appropriate compensation be paid for such work. Any other conclusion would deprive the iron ore miners of the just remuneration guaranteed them by the Act for contributing their time, liberty, and strength *primarily for the benefit of others*" (my emphasis).

3. The question of entrepreneurial control is also important. See, e.g., Restate-ment of Employment Law § 1.01(b) (Am. Law Inst. 2015): "An individual renders services as an independent businessperson and not as an employee

when the individual in his or her own interest exercises entrepreneurial control over important business decisions, including whether to hire and where to assign assistants, whether to purchase and where to deploy equipment, and whether and when to provide service to other customers." And yet, for example, members of a cooperative, who collectively own a business, never have *individual* entrepreneurial control over their actions.

4. The Court, with this quote, was interpreting the Fair Labor Standards Act. *Tony and Susan Alamo Foundation v. Secretary of Labor.*

5. Environmental Working Group, "USDA Subsidies in the United States Totaled $322.7 Billion from 1995–2014," n.d., https://farm.ewg.org/progdetail .php?fips=00000&progcode=total&page=conc, accessed October 3, 2016.

6. *Bobilin v. Board of Education, State of Hawaii,* 403 F. Supp. 1095 (D. Haw. 1975), http://law.justia.com/cases/federal/district-courts/FSupp/403/1095 /1568389/, accessed October 3, 2016.

7. See, e.g., Janelle Orsi, *Practicing Law in the Sharing Economy: Helping People Build Cooperatives, Social Enterprise, and Local Sustainable Economies* (Chicago: ABA Publishing, 2012), p. 377.

8. 29 U.S.C. § 203(e)(1).

9. Sarah Han, "Oakland Food Startup Josephine Announces It Will Shut Down Operations," Berkeleyside, February 2, 2018, www.berkeleyside.com /2018/02/02/josephine-announces-it-will-close/.

10. *Cotter v. Lyft, Inc.,* 60 F. Supp. 3d 1067, 1081 (N.D. Cal. 2015).

11. Ibid.

12. In legal theory as well as in common law, most exchanges, loosely defined, can be placed within one of two boxes: commercial and private. See, e.g., Adolf A. Berle, "Property, Production, and Revolution," *Columbia Law Review* 65, no. 1 (January 1965): 1–20, doi:10.2307/1120512.

13. Aaron Smith, "Shared, Collaborative, and On Demand: The New Digital Economy," Pew Research Center, May 19, 2016, www.pewinternet.org/2016 /05/19/the-new-digital-economy/, accessed December 1, 2016.

14. Marcel Mauss, *The Gift: The Form and Reason for Exchange in Archaic Societies,* trans. W. D. Halls (New York: Martino Fine Books, 2011).

Chapter 3: The Promise of Access

1. Kate Dean, "Farmland Changing Hands: A Study of Innovative Land Transfer Strategies," Cascade Harvest Coalition, Washington, November 2011,

www.cascadeharvest.org/files/u1/Farmland_Changing_Hands_0.pdf, accessed December 25, 2016.

2. "Succession Planning: Steps for a Sound Transition," Agribank, September 2015, http://info.agribank.com/agrithought/Pages/Succession-Planning .aspx, accessed February 5, 2017.

3. Adam Calo, "For Farmers, This Land Is Often Someone Else's," *San Francisco Chronicle*, October 28, 2016, www.sfchronicle.com/opinion/article/For -farmers-this-land-is-often-someone-else-s-10420689.php, accessed December 25, 2016.

4. Ibid.

5. Juli Obudzinski, "Beginning Farmer Policy Options for the Next Farm Bill," *Choices*, 4th quarter 2016, www.choicesmagazine.org/choices-magazine /theme-articles/theme-overview-addressing-the-challenges-of-entry-into -farming/beginning-farmer-policy-options-for-the-next-farm-bill.

6. Jason Henderson and Nathan Kauffman, "Farm Investment and Leverage Cycles: Will This Time Be Different?," *Federal Reserve Bank of Kansas City Economic Review* (2nd quarter 2013): 89–114, www.kansascityfed.org/publicat /econrev/pdf/13q2Henderson.pdf.

7. Barry K. Goodwin and François Ortalo Magné, "The Capitalization of Wheat Subsidies into Agricultural Land Values," *Canadian Journal of Agricultural Economics / Revue canadienne d'agroéconomie* 40, no. 1 (March 1992): 37–54, doi:10.1111/j.1744-7976.1992.tb03676.x; Laure Latruffe and Chantal Le Mouël, "Capitalization of Government Support in Agricultural Land Prices: What Do We Know?," *Journal of Economic Surveys* 23, no. 4 (September 2009): 659–691, doi:10.1111/j.1467-6419.2009.00575.x.

8. Andrew Gunnoe, "The Political Economy of Institutional Landownership: Neorentier Society and the Financialization of Land," *Rural Sociology* 79, no. 4 (December 2014): 478–504, doi:10.1111/ruso.12045.

9. Henderson and Kauffman, "Farm Investment and Leverage Cycles," p. 89.

10. Wendong Zhang, "Who Owns and Rents Iowa's Farmland?," File C2-78, December 2015, www.extension.iastate.edu/agdm/wholefarm/pdf/c2-78. pdf, accessed December 26, 2016.

11. Environmental Working Group, "Corn Subsidies in the United States Totaled $94.3 billion from 1995–2014," n.d., https://farm.ewg.org/progdetail .php?fips=00000&progcode=corn.

12. Kelliann Blazek et al., "Federal Enhanced Tax Deduction for Food Donation: A Legal Guide," Harvard Food Law and Policy Clinic, April 2016, www.chlpi.org/wp-content/uploads/2013/12/Food-Donation-Fed-Tax-Guide-for-Pub-2.pdf, accessed February 9, 2017.

13. See, e.g., Michael Carolan, *The Sociology of Food and Agriculture* (New York: Routledge, 2016).

14. Jacob Gersen, "The Single Bad Reason We Waste Billions of Pounds of Food," *Time*, August 24, 2016, http://time.com/4463449/food-waste-laws/, accessed February 9, 2017.

15. Hannah Levintova, "Is Giving Food to the Homeless Illegal in Your City Too?," *Mother Jones*, November 13, 2014, www.motherjones.com/politics/2014/11/90-year-old-florida-veteran-arrested-feeding-homeless-bans, accessed February 9, 2017.

16. Charlie Taylor, "FoodCloud Teams Up with Waitrose as It Expands in UK," *Irish Times*, January 19, 2017, www.irishtimes.com/business/technology/foodcloud-teams-up-with-waitrose-as-it-expands-in-uk-1.2941548, accessed February 9, 2017.

17. Luke Runyon, "Can the 'Airbnb of Kitchens' Give Local Food a Boost?," KUNC, National Public Radio, August 16, 2016, www.kunc.org/post/can-airbnb-kitchens-give-local-food-boost, accessed October 14, 2016.

18. "How the Food Corridor Works," www.thefoodcorridor.com/, accessed October 14, 2016.

19. Margaret Jane Radin, "Property and Personhood," *Stanford Law Review* 34, no. 5 (May 1982): 957–1015 (quotation on p. 986), doi:10.2307/1228541.

20. See also Adolf A. Berle, "Property, Production, and Revolution," *Columbia Law Review* 65, no. 1 (January 1965): 1–20, doi:10.2307/1120512.

21. Radin, "Property and Personhood," 1001.

22. Shelly Kreiczer-Levy, "Consumption Property in the Sharing Economy," *Pepperdine Law Review* 43, no. 1 (2016): 61–124, https://digitalcommons.pepperdine.edu/plr/vol43/iss1/2.

23. Shelly Kreiczer-Levy, "Share, Own, Access" (November 8, 2015), *Yale Law & Policy Review* 36 (2017): 155–218, doi:10.2139/ssrn.2777119, accessed October 14, 2016.

24. Ibid., 196.

25. Rachel Botsman and Roo Rogers, *What's Mine Is Yours: The Rise of Collaborative Consumption* (New York: HarperCollins, 2010).

26. See, e.g., Runyon, "The 'Airbnb of Kitchens.'"
27. Mark S. Granovetter, "The Strength of Weak Ties," *American Journal of Sociology* 78, no. 6 (May 1973): 1360–1380, doi:10.1086/225469.

Chapter 4: Social Trade-offs

1. See, e.g., Jake Zuckerman, "Machinery Link: Where Uber Meets Agriculture," *Northern Virginia Daily*, June 23, 2016, www.nvdaily.com/news/2016/06/hold-machinery-link-solutions-where-uber-meets-agriculture/, accessed September 28, 2016; Andrea Peterson, "Meet the Site That Is Like Uber—but for Tractors," *Washington Post*, May 6, 2016, www.washington post.com/news/the-switch/wp/2016/05/06/meet-the-site-that-is-like-uber-but-for-tractors/, accessed September 28, 2016.
2. Jesse Newman, "U.S. Farm Income to Fall to Lowest Levels in Nine Years," *Wall Street Journal*, August 25, 2015, www.wsj.com/articles/u-s-farm-income-to-fall-to-lowest-level-in-nine-years-1440521337, accessed January 7, 2016.
3. Fleura Bardhi and Giana M. Eckhardt, "Access-Based Consumption: The Case of Car Sharing," *Journal of Consumer Research* 39, no. 4 (December 2012): 881–898, doi:10.1086/666376.
4. See, e.g., Arun Sundararajan, *The Sharing Economy: The End of Employment and the Rise of Crowd-Based Capitalism* (Cambridge, MA: MIT Press, 2016).
5. Brigit Helms and Anabella Palacios, 2016. "The Sharing Economy Can Transform Economic Development," *HuffPost* (blog), June 1, 2016, www.huffingtonpost.com/fomin/the-sharing-economy-can-t_b_10242948.html, accessed May 19, 2017.
6. Jarrett Bellini, "The No. 1 Thing to Consider before Opening a Restaurant," CNBC, March 15, 2016, www.cnbc.com/2016/01/20/heres-the-real-reason-why-most-restaurants-fail.html, accessed May 10, 2017.
7. See www.bbc.com/news/av/world-us-canada-37230916/drug-dealers-criminals-rapists-what-trump-thinks-of-mexicans.

Chapter 5: Putting Shared Technologies to Work

1. David Bennett, "U.S. Seed Law History: A Primer," Delta Farm Press, March 2, 2006, www.deltafarmpress.com/us-seed-law-history-primer, accessed December 18, 2016.
2. Ibid.

3. U.S. Department of Agriculture, National Institute of Food and Agriculture, "Corn Breeding: Lessons from the Past," Plant and Soil Sciences eLibrary, 2018, http://passel.unl.edu/pages/informationmodule.php?id informationmodule=1075412493&topicorder=10&maxto=12.

4. Naomi Creason, "Department of Agriculture Cracks Down on Seed Libraries," *Sentinel* (Carlisle, PA), July 31, 2014, http://cumberlink.com/news /local/communities/carlisle/department-of-agriculture-cracks-down-on -seed-libraries/article_8b0323f4-18f6-11e4-b4c1-0019bb2963f4.html, accessed December 21, 2016.

5. For details about the legislation, see https://leginfo.legislature.ca.gov/faces /billTextClient.xhtml?bill_id=201520160AB1810.

6. Pesticide Action Network, "A Win for Seed Diversity in California," Seed Freedom, October 12, 2016, http://seedfreedom.info/a-win-for-seed-diversity -in-california/.

7. These reflect 2016 events pulled from the organization's website, www.seed savers.org/, accessed October 24, 2016.

8. "The Open Source Seed Initiative," http://osseeds.org/, accessed December 22, 2016.

9. Sarah Shemkus, "Fighting the Seed Monopoly: 'We Want to Make Free Seed a Sort of Meme,'" *Guardian* (US edition), May 2, 2014, www.theguard ian.com/sustainable-business/seed-monopoly-free-seeds-farm-monsanto -dupont.

10. "American Farm Bureau Survey Shows Big Data Use Increasing, Big Questions Remain," American Farm Bureau Federation, Newsroom, October 20, 2014, www.fb.org/newsroom/american-farm-bureau-survey-shows -big-data-use-increasing-big-questions-rem.

Chapter 6: Overcoming Barriers

1. W. J. Spillman, "The Agricultural Ladder," *American Economic Review* 9, no. 1 (March 1919): 170–179, www.jstor.org/stable/1813998.

2. See, e.g., Jack R. Kloppenburg Jr. and Charles C. Geisler, "The Agricultural Ladder: Agrarian Ideology and the Changing Structure of U.S. Agriculture," *Journal of Rural Studies* 1, no. 1 (1985): 59–72, doi:10.1016/0743 -0167(85)90091-9.

3. Michael S. Carolan, *Embodied Food Politics* (Burlington, VT: Ashgate, 2011).

4. See, e.g., Shoshanah Inwood, Jill K. Clark, and Molly Bean, "The Differing Values of Multigeneration and First Generation Farmers: Their Influence on the Structure of Agriculture at the Rural Urban Interface," *Rural Sociology* 78, no. 3 (September 2013): 346–370, doi:10.1111/ruso.12012.

5. Carol Simpson, "Agriculture Research Project: Waterloo Wellington," Government of Ontario, Canada, December 2015, http://workforceplanningboard.com/Files/English/Agriculture_Research_final.pdf, accessed March 5, 2017.

6. The Farmers Guild home page, www.farmersguild.org/, accessed March 5, 2017.

7. "Iowa Corn: Who We Are," www.iowacorn.org/about/, accessed March 5, 2017.

8. U.S. Department of Agriculture, Farm Service Agency, "Minority and Women Farmers and Ranchers," www.fsa.usda.gov/programs-and-services/farm-loan-programs/minority-and-women-farmers-and-ranchers/index, accessed March 5, 2017.

9. Michael Carolan, *The Sociology of Food and Agriculture* (New York: Routledge, 2016).

10. See, e.g., Jo Little, "Rural Geography: Rural Gender Identity and the Performance of Masculinity and Femininity in the Countryside," *Progress in Human Geography* 26, no. 5 (2002): 665–670, doi:10.1191/0309132502ph394pr; Michael S. Carolan, "Barriers to the Adoption of Sustainable Agriculture on Rented Land: An Examination of Contesting Social Fields," *Rural Sociology* 70, no. 3 (September 2005): 387–413, doi:10.1526/0036011054831233.

11. Adam Calo, "For Farmers, This Land Is Often Someone Else's," *San Francisco Chronicle*, October 28, 2016, www.sfchronicle.com/opinion/article/For-farmers-this-land-is-often-someone-else-s-10420689.php, accessed December 25, 2016.

12. U.S. Department of Agriculture, Census of Agriculture, "2012 Census Highlights: Farm Demographics—U.S. Farmers by Gender, Age, Race, Ethnicity, and More," ACH12-3, May 2014, www.agcensus.usda.gov/Publications/2012/Online_Resources/Highlights/Farm_Demographics/, accessed March 5, 2017.

13. Steven B. Emery, "Independence and Individualism: Conflated Values in Farmer Cooperation?," *Agriculture and Human Values* 32, no. 1 (March 2015): 47–61, doi:10.1007/s10460-014-9520-8.

14. See, e.g., Margaret Alston, "Rural Male Suicide in Australia," *Social Science & Medicine* 74, no. 4 (February 2012): 515–522, doi:10.1016/j.so cscimed.2010.04.036; Lia Bryant and Bridget Garnham, "The Fallen Hero: Masculinity, Shame, and Farmer Suicide in Australia," *Gender, Place & Culture* 22, no. 1 (2015): 67–82, doi:10.1080/0966369X.2013.855628; Mensah Adinkrah, "Better Dead than Dishonored: Masculinity and Male Suicidal Behavior in Contemporary Ghana," *Social Science & Medicine* 74, no. 4 (February 2012): 474–481, doi:10.1016/j.socscimed.2010 .10.011.

15. See, e.g., Krystal D'Costa, "Why Don't People Return Their Shopping Carts?," *Scientific American,* April 26, 2017, https://blogs.scientificamerican .com/anthropology-in-practice/why-dont-people-return-their-shopping -carts/.

16. Jonathan T. Rothwell and Pablo Diego-Rosell, "Explaining Nationalist Political Views: The Case of Donald Trump," November 2, 2016, doi: 10.2139/ssrn.2822059, http://papers.ssrn.com/sol3/papers.cfm?abstract_id =2822059, accessed September 25, 2016.

Chapter 7: Walls Make Terrible Neighbors

1. Rachel Botsman, "The Case for Collaborative Consumption," filmed May 2010 in Sydney, Australia, TED video, 16:28, www.ted.com/talks/rachel _botsman_the_case_for_collaborative_consumption, accessed November 25, 2016.

2. As quoted in Sarah Kessler, "The 'Sharing Economy' Is Dead, and We Killed It," *Fast Company,* September 14, 2015, www.fastcompany.com/3050775/the -sharing-economy-is-dead-and-we-killed-it, accessed November 24, 2016.

3. Ibid.

4. Michael Carolan, "More than Active Food Citizens: A Longitudinal and Comparative Study of Alternative and Conventional Eaters," *Rural Sociology* 82, no. 2 (June 2017): 197–225, doi:10.1111/ruso.12120.

5. Barbara Gray and Jennifer J. Kish-Gephart, "Encountering Social Class Differences at Work: How 'Class Work' Perpetuates Inequality," *Academy of Man-*

agement Review 38, no. 4 (October 2013): 670–699, doi:10.5465/amr.2012 .0143; Michael W. Kraus et al., "Social Class, Solipsism, and Contextualism: How the Rich Are Different from the Poor," *Psychological Review* 119, no. 3 (July 2012): 546–572, doi:10.1037/a0028756.

6. See, e.g., Agata Gasiorowska et al., "Money Cues Increase Agency and Decrease Prosociality among Children: Early Signs of Market-Mode Behaviors," *Psychological Science* 27, no. 3 (March 2016): 331–344, doi:10.1177 /0956797615620378; Ashley V. Whillans, Eugene M. Caruso, and Elizabeth W. Dunn, "Both Selfishness and Selflessness Start with the Self: How Wealth Shapes Responses to Charitable Appeals," *Journal of Experimental Social Psychology* 70 (May 2017): 242–250, doi:10.1016/j.jesp.2016.11.009.

Chapter 8: From Pricks to Partners

1. "Bread and Stuff" is a pseudonym. Ensuring the anonymity of individuals meant also ensuring the anonymity of their businesses.

2. Gary S. Corner and Andrew P. Meyer, Federal Reserve Bank of St. Louis, "Community Bank Lending during the Financial Crisis," *Central Banker*, Spring 2013, www.stlouisfed.org/Publications/Central-Banker/Spring-2013 /Community-Bank-Lending-during-the-Financial-Crisis, accessed November 10, 2016.

3. See, e.g., Karen Gordon Mills and Brayden McCarthy, "The State of Small Business Lending: Credit Access during the Recovery and How Technology May Change the Game," Harvard Business School Working Paper 15-004, July 22, 2014, www.hbs.edu/faculty/Publication%20Files/15-004_09b1b f8b-eb2a-4e63-9c4e-0374f770856f.pdf, accessed November 10, 2016.

4. Garrett Martin and Amar Patel, Maine Center for Economic Policy, "Going Local: Quantifying the Economic Impacts of Buying from Locally Owned Businesses in Portland, Maine," December 5, 2011, www.mecep .org/view.asp?news=2003, accessed November 8, 2016.

5. Civic Economics, "Indie Impact Study Series: A National Comparative Survey with the American Booksellers Association," Summer 2012, http://nebula .wsimg.com/09d4a3747498c7e97b42657484cae80d?AccessKeyId =8E410A17553441C49302&disposition=0&alloworigin=1, accessed November 8, 2016.

6. David S. Brown, "Discounting Democracy: Wal-Mart, Social Capital, Civic Engagement, and Voter Turnout in the United States," September 9,

2009, http://ssrn.com/abstract=1398946, doi:10.2139/ssrn.1398946, accessed November 8, 2016.

7. Ibid., 4.

8. Stephan J. Goetz and Anil Rupasingha, "Wal-Mart and Social Capital," *American Journal of Agricultural Economics* 88, no. 5 (December 2006): 1304–1310, doi:10.1111/j.1467-8276.2006.00949.x.

9. Michael Carolan, *Cheaponomics: The High Cost of Low Prices* (New York: Routledge, 2014).

10. See, e.g., Kevin M. Leyden, "Social Capital and the Built Environment: The Importance of Walkable Neighborhoods," *American Journal of Public Health* 93, no. 9 (September 2003): 1546–1551, doi:10.2105/AJPH.93 .9.1546; Tomoya Hanibuchi et al., "Does Walkable Mean Sociable? Neighborhood Determinants of Social Capital among Older Adults in Japan," *Health & Place* 18, no. 2 (March 2012): 229–239, doi:10.1016/j.healthplace .2011.09.015.

11. Michael S. Carolan, *No One Eats Alone: Food as a Social Enterprise* (Washington, DC: Island Press, 2017).

12. Emily Maltby, "Small Biz Loan Failure Rate Hits 12%," CNNMoney, February 25, 2009, http://money.cnn.com/2009/02/25/smallbusiness/smallbiz _loan_defaults_soar.smb/, accessed November 11, 2016.

13. See, e.g., Alessandra Cassar, Luke Crowley, and Bruce Wydick, "The Effect of Social Capital on Group Loan Repayment: Evidence from Field Experiments," *Economic Journal* 117, no. 517 (February 2007): F85–F106, doi:10 .1111/j.1468-0297.2007.02016.x.

14. Kathleen D. Vohs, Nicole N. Mead, and Miranda R. Goode, "The Psychological Consequences of Money," *Science* 314, no. 5802 (November 17, 2006): 1154–1156, doi:10.1126/science.1132491.

15. Yuwei Jiang, Zhansheng Chen, and Robert S. Wyer Jr., "Impact of Money on Emotional Expression," *Journal of Experimental Social Psychology* 55 (November 2014): 228–233, doi:10.1016/j.jesp.2014.07.013.

Chapter 9: Food Sovereignty

1. Raymond Williams, *Keywords: A Vocabulary of Culture and Society* (Oxford: Oxford University Press, 1985).

2. These are actual self-descriptions taken from interviews with members of the cooperative.

3. Steven B. Emery, "Independence and Individualism: Conflated Values in Farmer Cooperation?," *Agriculture and Human Values* 32, no. 1 (March 2015): 47–61, doi:10.1007/s10460-014-9520-8.

4. Marshall McLuhan, *Understanding Media: The Extensions of Man* (New York: McGraw-Hill, 1964).

Index

Page numbers followed by "f" and "t" indicate figures and tables.